GROUP'S BLOCKBUSTER MOVIE EVENTS

Relevant Retreats and Movie Nights

FOR YOUTH MINISTRY

Bryan Belknap

Group

Loveland, Colorado

Acknowledgments

Thank you...

Debbie Gowensmith for making a good book great.

Act One for helping me perfect my craft.

Kathy Dietrich for pushing me to be the best writer possible.

Dedicated to...

My bride, Jill, for always supporting me.

Our joyful son, Cash, for keeping us laughing.

Group's Blockbuster Movie Events

Copyright © 2005 Bryan Belknap

Visit our Web site: **www.group.com**

Credits

Editor: Debbie Gowensmith
Creative Development Editors: Kate S. Holburn and Mikal Keefer
Chief Creative Officer: Joani Schultz
Copy Editor: Billie Hunteman
Art Director: Nancy Serbus
Cover Art Director/Designer: Jeff Storm
Cover Photographer: Rodney Stewart
Illustrator: Mitch Mortimer
Production Manager: Dodie Tipton

Library of Congress Cataloging-in-Publication Data
Belknap, Bryan.
    Group's blockbuster movie events : relevant retreats and movie nights for
youth ministry / by Bryan Belknap. -- 1st American pbk. ed.
        p. cm.
ISBN 0-7644-2759-8 (pbk. : alk. paper)
 1. Church work with youth. 2. Spiritual retreats for youth. 3.
Motion--Religious aspects--Christianity. 4. Film criticism. I. Group
Publishing. II. Title.
 BV4447.B45 2005
 268'.67--dc22
                                                        2005005069

10 9 8 7 6 5 4 3 2 1   14 13 12 11 10 09 08 07 06 05
Printed in the United States of America.

Contents

Introduction

Movies in church? Why?!

"Movies teach as Jesus taught." That's what I tell people when they question my sanity in bringing Hollywood inside the church. (And by "church," I mean a building—not the biblical view of the church as people. By the biblical definition, "the church" goes to movies all the time!) The naysayers presume that using movies in youth ministry is lazy, seeking to entertain rather than to study Scripture. Sober judgment, however, leads to the realization that movies are modern parables. Jesus used parables to impart deep spiritual truths in a way that connected with people's daily lives. Jesus talked so much about fishing, talents, and tax collectors so that people would understand and remember those spiritual truths.

Like it or not, modern-day life doesn't include sheep, slaves, and seeds. The teen world consists of school, text messaging, and comic book heroes. If Jesus arrived in the flesh on earth today (well, it would be the Second Coming, but I digress), he would create parables using the stuff of modern culture to make known the kingdom of God. That 21st-century language incorporates film—its characters, themes, and imagination. Unfortunately, Christians have been sending young people out into the world completely unprepared for dealing with this cultural force or its messages. They can't discern truth from lies and, more tragically, they don't see how their faith could possibly connect with "real" life.

To be quite honest, *Group's Blockbuster Movie Events* wants to *immerse* your teens in the Bible. Experiencing an event such as a theme night helps your young people actually *live* abstract spiritual concepts. The movie they watch becomes a vehicle for diving deep into God's Word. The event, utilizing the movie, explores God's eternal truth and connects that truth to everyday life rather than distracting from or dumbing down the truth.

More importantly, these events teach teenagers about God in a way they will actually remember. They embed the gospel within the culture, getting outside the church walls and into your students' everyday lives. After experiencing these events, your young people will think about God's command to serve others every time they see a picture of Spider-Man and will remember to have loving compassion toward others any time they hear Lindsay Lohan's voice. This book helps you teach lessons that last a lifetime—whether or not your teenagers want to remember the lessons!

Even if someone has seen one of these movies a hundred times, it will feel fresh and new as a movie event. Unforgettable, active-learning experiences that point young people to God—such as skits, games, and prayer stations—surround each film. Your students never will have watched these movies from the biblical perspective that these events encourage, and they'll never be able to see these movies again without remembering the spiritual lessons. Using this book helps you subvert the culture and transform it into something redemptive.

What About the Bad Stuff?

Many people argue about inappropriate content in films. Even if the message is good, one profane word renders the movie *verboten*. First, as I'm sure you've noticed, the Bible doesn't whitewash human nature. You have fornication, bloody murder, and betrayal…and that's just Genesis! God left the ugliness of humanity in the Holy Scriptures for a reason. (And no, it wasn't to add excitement.) You see—and this is important—seeing or hearing about sinful activity is not sin. *Not learning* from the sinful behavior of others and committing the same offensive actions *is*. (Read that again slowly to make sure I'm not writing blasphemy.)

So be upfront with your young people. Let them know when coarse language or uncomfortable situations will be portrayed. Acknowledge that the world is a messy place, which is why Jesus had to die on the cross for our sin. Be clear with your group that you are not condoning or promoting any sinful behavior that occurs in these movies. Frame discussions around the idea that by seeing people make poor choices, we can learn how to avoid those same mistakes.

Besides, good drama is born from people making mistakes. If no one does anything bad, no one changes; then no one learns lessons to pass on to the audience. Jim Carrey's character in *Bruce Almighty* had to display selfish, immoral behavior in the beginning. Otherwise, his character wouldn't need to grow or learn anything new to become a better person. Many explicitly Christian movies feel unbelievable because they portray perfect people making perfect choices for the perfect outcome…and that's why they are perfectly boring.

That said, *you must preview each movie yourself*. I have identified in general terms what might cause some raised eyebrows. Every church, however, is different. What may be acceptable to show at my church in Los Angeles may not fly in my childhood church in Texas. One church isn't better than the other, but they minister to different cultures. Your personal church community may find a scene with, for example, alcohol in it particularly offensive. That's why *you must preview the movies*. Identify potential hazards and determine the best ways of handling them. You can address them before the screening, skip the scenes entirely, or bleep out the "potty" parts through editing.

Protect Yourself

One of the best ways to deflect potential criticism is through permission slips. Parents are amazing creatures. They can split you in two with their tongues a nanosecond after learning what you've "done" to their children, but they gladly chaperone the very same event given a little advanced warning. Simply by alerting parents to what's going to take place, you'll find yourself with allies rather than a lynch mob. I've supplied a sample permission letter at the end of this introduction to serve as a possible template.

Copyright Law

In general, federal copyright laws do not allow you to use videos or DVDs (even ones you own) for any purpose other than home viewing. Though some exceptions allow for the use of short segments of copyrighted material for educational purposes, it's best to be on the safe side. Your church can obtain a license from Christian Video Licensing for a small fee. Just visit www.cvli.org or call 1-888-302-6020 for more information. When using a movie that is not covered by the license, we recommend directly contacting the movie studio to seek permission for use of the clip.

What's in Each Event?

Each event should run between 185 and 210 minutes. Each chapter includes the following sections (named after the different stages of making a Hollywood movie):

The Pitch—A brief overview of the theme and what your students will learn

Favorite Quote—The focus verse

More Quotables—All Scripture used during the event

The Props—A list of all the supplies you'll need

Movie Review—A synopsis of the movie and the spiritual connection that will be made

Pastoral Guidance—A broad overview of potentially offensive material in the movie

Preproduction—Everything you'll need to do to prepare and set up before your students arrive

Bonus Swag—Ideas for creating the movie's ambience through décor, costumes, music, and so on

The Red Carpet—The initial impressions participants will receive upon entering and any activities that take place prior to watching the movie

The Production—Viewing the movie

Postproduction—Activities that take place after the movie ends

Word of Mouth—A final activity or "take-away" that will help students carry the event into their everyday lives

One Sheets—All the reproducible handouts necessary for the event

Suggested Overnight Retreat Schedule—Suggestions for expanding the event into an overnight retreat

www.group.com/blockbusterevents—A special Web site full of creative materials you can use to promote these movie events.

Action!

After you experience all of these movie events, your creative juices should be overflowing so much that *you* will be writing movie events of your very own for some of your favorite movies. Instead of watching the *Princess Bride* for the thousandth time, you can transform it into a study on commitment. (Hmm, there's one for volume two!)

Stop letting movies dictate the message, shouting an incorrect worldview while your teenagers passively soak it in with their popcorn. *Group's Blockbuster Movie Events* teaches young people how to dialogue about each film, evaluate where it agrees with or contradicts their faith, and accept or reject those messages. Training Christians to view media through a Jesus lens that filters out the bad stuff while connecting faith more tightly to everyday life is a skill that pays dividends for a lifetime.

For more great ideas on subverting pop culture and using it to create biblical illustrations, check out www.MinistryAndMedia.com. Every week I review a current movie, DVD, and CD (both Christian and secular), providing related Scripture-based discussion starters. Also, if you're looking for video-clip illustrations for Bible studies or sermons, check out *Group's Blockbuster Movie Illustrations* and *Group's Blockbuster Movie Illustrations: The Sequel.* Thank you so much for buying this book. I know your students will never be able to look at movies the same way again. God bless your ministry!

Suggested Schedule

January—*Seabiscuit* (New Year's)

February—*A Walk to Remember* (Valentine's Day)

March—*Bruce Almighty* (Lent)

April—*Joshua* (Easter)

May—*Holes* (Memorial Day)

June—*Miracle* (mission trips/camp)

July—*Spider-Man 2* (Independence Day)

August—*The Mission* (back to school)

September—*The Emperor's Club* (coping with school)

October—*Signs* (Halloween)

November—*Freaky Friday* (Thanksgiving)

December—*Finding Nemo* (Christmas)

Sample Permission Letter

Jesus taught deep spiritual truths with examples from everyday life. The dominant form of modern parable is film. In an effort to connect teenagers' everyday lives with their faith while illustrating spiritual matters in a concrete way they'll remember, I would like to host a Movie Event. We will be watching the movie _____

_____ to learn about

_____. I've carefully screened every movie, so I must warn you that this film contains

_____. I assure you, though, that the focus always will remain on God's Word. Young people will learn spiritual truth in a way they can never forget. My prayer is to bring Scripture alive and get teenagers thinking—and living—their faith.

Please contact me with any questions or concerns about showing this movie. Please sign below if you grant permission for your teenager to watch the movie during the Movie Event. Thank you for your time and your trust with your child's spiritual growth!

Blessings,

Your signature

Legal Guardian's Signature _____

Date _____

The Props:

☐ *Bibles*
☐ *movie: Bruce Almighty*
☐ *DVD player or VCR*
☐ *TV or video projector*
☐ *inflatable globes (You can find these at a travel store, many children's stores, and through online catalogs.)*
☐ *thin sheet of metal*
☐ *air mattress*
☐ *blue bedsheet*
☐ *modeling clay*
☐ *bullhorn or microphone*
☐ *" 'Family of God Feud' Game Boards" (p. 14)*
☐ *computer with PowerPoint and a projector (optional)*
☐ *poster board*
☐ *marker*
☐ *tape*
☐ *newsprint*
☐ *pens or pencils*
☐ *1 "Penciling in God" handout (p. 15) for each person*
☐ *supplies to make bracelets—beads, leather cord, scissors, and other craft supplies*

Take 8
Blockbuster Movie Events

What If God Was One of Us?
Discovering God's Plan

The Pitch

Bruce Almighty shows, with hilarious effect, what would happen if a human being had God's powers. After watching this film, students will have a better understanding of God's character and how to build a relationship with God.

Favorite Quote

"Be still, and know that I am God; I will be exalted among the nations, I will be exalted in the earth" (Psalm 46:10).

More Quotables: Deuteronomy 6:4-12; Isaiah 40:28; Romans 1:18-23

Suggested Schedule

Section	Activities	Time	Supplies
The Red Carpet	*Introducing the Almighty!*	15-20 minutes	Bibles, inflatable globes, sheet of metal, air mattress, blue bedsheet, modeling clay, bullhorn or microphone
The Production	*Bruce Almighty*	105 minutes	Movie: *Bruce Almighty,* DVD player or VCR, TV
Postproduction	*Discussion*	5-10 minutes	
	Family of God Feud	25-35 minutes	Bibles, " 'Family of God Feud' Game Boards" handout (p. 14), poster board, tape, marker
	Penciling in God	15-20 minutes	Bible, "Penciling in God" handout (p. 15), pens or pencils
Word of Mouth	*Say a Little Prayer*	15-20 minutes	Bibles, computer with PowerPoint and projector or newsprint, tape, and marker; beads, leather cord, scissors

Movie Review

Bruce Almighty shows what happens when God (Morgan Freeman) endows newsman Bruce Nolan (Jim Carrey) with all his power. When Bruce is fired, mugged, and generally has the worst day of his life, he feels that God is against him. God answers this criticism by giving Bruce his job. Bruce proceeds to use his newly acquired omnipotence to serve his own selfish desires of gaining the anchor position at work; wooing his girlfriend, Grace (Jennifer Aniston); and fulfilling any other self-centered whim that comes his way. When his choices result in disastrous effects in his own life, throughout the city, and even across the globe, Bruce seeks God's mercy and submits himself to God's perfect will.

This movie constantly surprises me. That someone convinced Jim Carrey (and by extension Hollywood) to get on his knees and ask God to take control of his life will go down as one of the great cinematic miracles of our age. That *Bruce Almighty* also presents a mostly accurate picture of God, his powers, and his love for us earns the movie another gold star. (It helps that the director and writer are Christian. That doesn't make the movie pure, though. Read "Pastoral Guidance" for more on that.) Besides gales of laughter, your young people will be given a lot to think about concerning their heavenly Father. Through attending this event, your teenagers can better understand God's power and attributes and can learn how to make God a more integral part of their lives. As a result, teenagers will have greater confidence in God and will actively seek God's guidance regarding everyday life.

Pastoral Guidance

Though *Bruce Almighty* explores the nature of God with a redemptive and enlightening tone, it contains some scenes that definitely will fluster some deacons. Bruce flips off a co-worker (10:00) and even says the f-word (17:15). He also lives with his girlfriend, and we witness them preparing for a night of passion (43:45–44:30). These scenes all are played for big laughs, and they help the audience understand two things: (1) Bruce definitely has some flaws that need attention, and (2) God loves people regardless of the condition of their lives—despite their sin. This movie fights the concept that a person needs to become perfect *before* coming to God. *Bruce Almighty* says that God wants you "as is" and that getting to know God personally will help you change from the inside out. (See page 5 for more details, or visit www.screenit.com for a detailed list of the film's content.)

Preproduction

Set up a movie viewing area with the TV or projector and VCR or DVD player. Have the movie set up and ready to go.

Set out a few supplies with which participants can "play God" before you start the movie. For example, set out some inflatable globes, a thin sheet of metal, an air mattress that's partially blown up and covered with a blue sheet, and modeling clay.

Create two game boards to use during the "Family of God Feud" activity. Utilize

Take 9
Blockbuster
Movie Events

PowerPoint if you have the technology and skill, or use the old-fashioned method of writing on poster board. Use the "'Family of God Feud' Game Boards" sheet (p. 14) as a pattern. At the top of each piece of poster board, write one of the "Family of God Feud" questions. Below the question, write each possible answer in a rectangle. Cover the answers with pieces of paper or poster board that can be removed when the correct answers are given.

Create a PowerPoint slide with the words from Psalm 46:10 written on it: "Be still, and know that I am God; I will be exalted among the nations, I will be exalted in the earth." Project the slide on a wall. A low-tech alternative is to use newsprint and markers to create a banner to hang in the meeting area.

Bonus Swag

Use these ideas to produce even more of the movie's ambience throughout this event.
- *Set up a few mops with buckets around your meeting space.*
- *Cover colorful walls by taping or tacking up white sheets or newsprint where necessary.*
- *Hang inflatable globes around the room.*
- *Have volunteers and/or teenagers dress in all-white clothing.*

 **WEB SITE NOTE:** *Be sure to check out www.group.com/blockbusterevents for great resources to promote and plan these events!*

The Red Carpet

As participants arrive, direct them to the activities you've set up that allow them to "play God" before you start the movie. Your teenagers can hold the "world" in their hands, create the sound of thunder by wiggling the sheet metal back and forth, walk on "water" by walking over the sheet-covered mattress, and mold their own creations with the clay.

When everyone has arrived, call participants together.

Introducing the Almighty!

Say: **You may not realize it, but each of you was endowed with all of God's power when you entered this room. We want to hear how you're going to use it! Each of you will have the opportunity to proclaim to the group how you will use your new power. First, you'll introduce yourself by saying, "I am [your name] almighty!" Then you'll tell us what you're going to do with this power. I'll go first so you can see what I mean.**

Demonstrate the activity before allowing everyone else an opportunity. For example, I would say, "I am Bryan almighty, and I would have the Beatles rise from the dead and perform a private concert for me and all my friends."

Once the proclamations end, have teenagers break into groups of two or three to answer the following questions:

- *If your command really came true, what would be possible positive effects on the world? What would be possible negative effects?*
- *How do human beings sometimes act like they could do God's job? Why do you think we act this way?*

Have students read Isaiah 40:28 in their groups.
Ask: • *Would you want to be able to figure out God completely? Why or why not?*

Wrap up the discussion by saying: **We're going to see how one man handled having all of God's power. As we watch *Bruce Almighty*, see what you can learn about God's characteristics and abilities.**

The Production—*Bruce Almighty*

Gather everyone around the TV to watch the movie. Start the film, sit back, relax, and enjoy!

Postproduction

Discussion

When the movie ends, allow everyone to take a bathroom break. Once everyone is back together, ask:

- *Was there anything in the movie that you thought misrepresented God or contradicted God's Word?*
- Bruce Almighty *had a lot of good things to say about God. How do you think the movie accurately portrayed God?*
- *Did you learn anything new about God? Explain.*

Take time to discuss any questions your teenagers might have. Some of the movie's flippant statements can be misinterpreted, and its characters' choices can lead to incorrect assumptions.

After a few minutes of discussion, have participants move to the area where you set up the "Family of God Feud" game board.

Family of God Feud

Say: **We're going to test your newfound knowledge of the Creator. I need two volunteers up here right now!**

Once you have two volunteers, explain that each volunteer will represent half of the group. Reveal the "Family of God Feud" game board you created, and say: **We're all going to play Family of God Feud.** [Name] **will answer for this side of the room, and** [name] **will answer for the other side. You'll try to answer the questions based on what we learned from the movie.**

If your team guesses an answer that appears on our game board, your team can guess again until you give an answer that's not on the board. Then the other team gets to try. You get one point for each answer that appears on the game board, and your goal is to get the most points by the end. By the way, just because your answers don't appear on the board, it doesn't mean they're wrong—but you get points only for answers appearing on the game board.

When teenagers understand how to play, say: **Let's start the Family of God Feud!**

Have the two representatives face one another.

Ask: • *Who played the role of God in* Bruce Almighty*?*

The first representative to shout out the correct answer gets control of the board. Ask that representative's team one of the questions from the game board, and set a time limit of 10 seconds for discussion before the representative has to give the team's answer. If the answer appears on the game board, allow the team another 10 seconds to guess another answer. Continue until the team guesses an answer that doesn't appear on the game board. Then if all the answers on the game board haven't been revealed, ask the same question of the other team with 10 seconds for discussion between correct responses. When both teams have guessed all the answers or have guessed answers not appearing on the game board, reveal the rest of the answers. Encourage teenagers to shout out the answers as you reveal them. Then ask the other game board's question, starting with the team that guessed second for the previous question. Afterwards, congratulate both teams for a great game.

PRODUCTION TIP

If you have a large group, create more than one game board, and run the game simultaneously with multiple teams.

Ask: • *What have you learned about God's character so far tonight?*
- *How does this new knowledge change your perception of God?*

Have teenagers form groups of three and read aloud Romans 1:18-23 with their group members. Then have groups discuss the following questions:

- *Why do you think it can be difficult to get to know God, who is so "clearly seen"?*
- *What ideas for getting to know God better do these verses inspire?*
- *How do people "exchange" their knowledge of God for idols today?*
- *How can a person gain knowledge of God? How can a person tighten a relationship with God?*

Penciling in God

Have everyone gather back together, and say: **Obviously, God has a lot to offer us—knowledge, protection, blessings, guidance. God almost sounds like a Mafia godfather! Seriously, God wants to be part of each of our lives, but often we keep God at the periphery just as Bruce did.**

That's a mistake. We should include God in every area of our lives. When we don't, we run the risk of making mistakes that God would help us avoid.

Distribute a "Penciling in God" handout (p. 15) and a pen or pencil to each person.

Say: **We're going to find ways to keep God in the loop of our everyday lives so we don't mistakenly trust in "images." Listen carefully because you'll complete several steps. First, fill in your schedule from today** (or the last weekday) **on the handout. Then ask yourself whether you included God in those moments. Look over your schedule, and answer honestly to yourself. Then think about how things might have been different if God had been involved. Finally, write on your schedule a consistent time you can spend with God. Pencil God into your schedule.**

When everyone understands the instructions, ask teenagers to remain quiet while everyone works.

After 10 minutes or when the majority of students seem to be finished, have them return to their groups of three to discuss the following questions:

- *If you struggle to include God in your daily schedule, what's the main reason you struggle?*
- *How might turning to God throughout the day affect your daily schedule?*
- *What are some practical ways you can learn to incorporate God into every activity in your day? How will you try to make that happen this week?*

SPECIAL EFFECTS

While teenagers think and write, play Rebecca St. James' *God* CD or your own mix of songs that talk about God.

Word of Mouth
Say a Little Prayer

Say: **Hopefully you've learned a lot tonight about who God is and the relationship God hopes to have with you. That said, it's often easy to simply let other things shove God to the side since you can't really see him. God is not a family member who wants a hug, a textbook that has to be read, or a phone call that must be answered. God always is there, ready and waiting, but often is ignored.**

Jews have a very practical way for sparking their memory of God. They recite the Shema every morning and every evening. Part of the Shema comes from Deuteronomy chapter 6. Ask a volunteer to read aloud Deuteronomy 6:4-12.

Say: **Jews literally kept these verses strapped to their arms or attached to their doors. We're going to remind ourselves of God in a similar way—by making bracelets like the one Grace gave to Bruce. This prayer bracelet can help you think of God and the active part he wants to play in your life.**

Direct teenagers to the area where you've set out beads, leather cord, and other supplies for creating prayer bracelets.

Give students plenty of time to make their bracelets. When time is up, have everyone gather together.

Say: **When you see your bracelet, you can remember who you made it for and say a little prayer of commitment to God. The more you do that—the more time you spend connecting to the living God who made you and loves you dearly—the more clearly you will feel God's presence in your life. By doing that,**

you also live out God's command in Psalm 46:10.

Point out the banner or slide you created with the verse written out, and have teenagers read it aloud with you. Close in prayer for connection with and direction from God in the week ahead.

Suggested Overnight Retreat Schedule

If you'd like to extend this event into an overnight retreat, use this schedule as a starting point.

Day	Time	Activities	Supplies
Friday	7:00 p.m.-7:30 p.m.	Seat attendees	
	7:30 p.m.-9:15 p.m.	*Bruce Almighty*	Movie: *Bruce Almighty*, DVD or videotape player, TV
	9:15 p.m.-9:25 p.m.	*Discussion*	
	9:25 p.m.-10:15 p.m.	Snacks	
	10:15 p.m.-11:30 p.m.	Free time	
	Midnight	Lights out	
Saturday	8:00 a.m.-8:30 a.m.	Devotion	
	8:30 a.m.-9:00 a.m.	Breakfast	
	9:00 a.m.-10:00 a.m.	*Introducing the Almighty!*	Bibles, inflatable globes, sheet of metal, air mattress, bedsheet, clay, bullhorn
		Family of God Feud	Bibles," 'Family of God Feud' Game Boards" (p. 14), poster board, tape, marker
	10:00 a.m.-noon	Games or group activities	
	Noon-1:00 p.m.	Lunch	
	1:00 p.m.-3:00 p.m.	Free time	
	3:00 p.m.-4:00 p.m.	*Penciling in God*	Bible, "Penciling in God" handout (p. 15), pens or pencils
		Say a Little Prayer	Bibles, computer with PowerPoint and projector or newsprint, tape, and marker; beads, leather cord, scissors
	4:00 p.m.-5:00 p.m.	Free time	
	5:00 p.m.-6:00 p.m.	Dinner	
	6:00 p.m.-7:30 p.m.	Worship and prayer	
	7:30 p.m.-8:00 p.m.	Pack and leave	

"Family of God Feud" Game Boards

WHAT ARE THE CHARACTERISTICS OF GOD?

ALL-POWERFUL (OMNIPOTENT)	FORGIVING
ALL-KNOWING (OMNISCIENT)	HEARS AND ANSWERS PRAYER
WANTS A RELATIONSHIP WITH HUMANITY	WANTS US TO WILLINGLY SURRENDER OUR WILL TO HIS
DOESN'T FORCE PEOPLE TO LOVE HIM (CREATED FREE WILL)	MEETS PEOPLE WHERE THEY ARE
CREATOR	LOVING

WHAT MISCONCEPTIONS DID BRUCE HAVE ABOUT GOD?

GOD MAKES BAD THINGS HAPPEN TO PEOPLE.	GOD ENJOYS WATCHING PEOPLE SUFFER.
GOD DOESN'T CARE WHAT HAPPENS TO PEOPLE.	GOD IS DISTANT.
GOD DOESN'T ANSWER PEOPLE WHEN THEY PRAY.	

Penciling in God

*Today's Date*_____

6:00 AM	
6:30 AM	
7:00 AM	
7:30AM	
8:00 AM	
8:30 AM	
9:00 AM	
9:30 AM	
10:00 AM	
10:30 AM	
11:00 AM	
11:30 AM	
NOON	
12:30 PM	
1:00 PM	
1:30 PM	
2:00 PM	
2:30 PM	
3:00 PM	
3:30 PM	
4:00 PM	
4:30 PM	
5:00 PM	
5:30 PM	
6:00 PM	
6:30 PM	
7:00 PM	
7:30 PM	
8:00 PM	
8:30 PM	
9:00 PM	
9:30 PM	
10:00 PM	

Penciling in God

Movie:

The Emperor's Club
(Universal Pictures, 2002)

Rating:

PG-13 for some sexual content

The Props:

- ☐ *Bibles*
- ☐ *movie: The Emperor's Club*
- ☐ *DVD player or VCR*
- ☐ *TV or video projector*
- ☐ *masking tape*
- ☐ *newsprint*
- ☐ *marker*
- ☐ *easel*
- ☐ *large map of the U.S. mounted on corkboard or foam board*
- ☐ *throwing dart*
- ☐ *yardstick*
- ☐ *1 "Spin Zone" handout (p. 22)*
- ☐ *scissors*
- ☐ *1 "Following the Path" handout (p. 23) for each participant*
- ☐ *pens or pencils*

The End Depends on the Beginning:
Integrity Matters

The Pitch

The Emperor's Club presents a compelling case for making righteous decisions at a young age. Ignoring the "little" things like respect for those in authority or cheating on tests damages integrity and builds a character of compromise for the future.

Favorite Quote

"But seek first his kingdom and his righteousness, and all these things will be given to you as well" (Matthew 6:33).

More Quotables: Proverbs 4; Matthew 6:1-6, 33; 25:14-30; John 8:32; 2 Thessalonians 3:3-9; Hebrews 12:1-3

Suggested Schedule

Section	Activities	Time	Supplies
The Red Carpet	*The Spin Zone*	15-20 minutes	"Spin Zone" handout (p. 22), scissors
The Production	*The Emperor's Club*	105 minutes	Movie: *The Emperor's Club*, DVD player or VCR, TV
Postproduction	*Discussion*	10-15 minutes	Bibles
	How Did I Get Here?	20-25 minutes	Bibles, mounted U.S. map, easel, dart, marker, yardstick
	Following the Path	25-30 minutes	Bibles, newsprint, tape, marker, "Following the Path" handout (p. 23), pens or pencils
Word of Mouth	*Praying the Path*	10-15 minutes	Bible, masking tape

Take 16
Blockbuster Movie Events

Movie Review

The Emperor's Club presents the legacy of an honorable classics teacher, Mr. William Hundert (Kevin Kline), and his impact on one particular class of students. His regimented and well-behaved class faces complete disruption with the arrival of Sedgewick Bell (Emile Hirsch), a senator's son. This unruly young man attempts to sway the class away from the ideals of integrity and character, leaning instead toward disrespect, pranks, and anarchy. Mr. Hundert believes that learning from the great men of history produces great men, and the story reveals whether his lifelong passion bore any fruit.

This movie explores the abstract concept of integrity in vivid colors. Sedgewick makes what some excuse as "harmless" mistakes or normal acting out that's due to a strained relationship with his father, and he grows into a conniving, hypocritical man. Use this event as an opportunity for your students to raise the bar of their personal behavior—not only as an act of devotion to God, but also to build a life in which they can take pride. By the end of this experience, your young people will be convicted of personal gray areas they let slide and will be energized to create a life of integrity.

Pastoral Guidance

The Emperor's Club contains a half-dozen scattered profanities and shows Sedgewick flipping off Mr. Hundert (30:30). Also be aware of scenes in which some students look at pornographic magazines (22:30) and prepare to engage in skinny-dipping (27:00). None of these scenes are gratuitous, however. Not only do the students suffer consequences for their actions, but these scenes also support the theme of small choices making a big impact on future character. (See page 5 for more details or visit www.screenit.com for a detailed list of the film's content.)

Preproduction

In all of your advertising and announcements, make it clear that each student should bring a bedsheet he or she can wear as a toga. Emphasize that this is *not* a toga party, though; teenagers should wear everyday clothing and merely drape their makeshift togas on top (see illustration for an example of how to drape a toga effectively). Including this information has the side benefit of generating excitement about the event.

Set up a movie viewing area with the TV or projector and VCR or DVD player. Have the movie set up and ready to go.

Tape a sheet of newsprint to a wall. You'll use it during the "Follow the Path" activity to write down suggested names.

Use an easel to stand up a large map of the United States that's mounted on corkboard or some other substance that will hold darts.

> **PRODUCTION TIP**
>
> If possible, have a few extra bedsheets on hand for those who forget their togas.

Students will be throwing darts at the map, and you don't want to have to explain to the deacons why there are dozens of tiny holes in the wall! Set a yardstick near the map, and use a marker to indicate the location of your town and a city across the country from your town.

Photocopy the "Spin Zone" handout (p. 22), and cut it into six squares as indicated.

Use masking tape to create a path on the floor of your meeting room. You can make the path as compact or lengthy as you wish. For example, you can create a path that circles inside the walls of your meeting room or even a maze with a different entrance and exit. Students will pray as they walk this path, so make it long enough for them to offer a significant prayer.

Bonus Swag

Use these ideas to produce even more of the movie's ambience throughout this event.

- *Convert your meeting room into a classroom for the classics, complete with busts and statues of ancient philosophers and leaders such as Plato, Julius Caesar, Alexander the Great, and Socrates.*
- *Cover a chalkboard with famous quotes from history's great thinkers. You can find quotation books at the library or quotes at www.quotationspage.com, www.brainyquote.com and www.bartleby.com.*
- *Stack textbooks around the meeting area.*
- *Hang maps of the ancient world—which you can copy from world history books or encyclopedias—on the walls.*
- *Create and distribute one Caesar-style leaf crown (laurel wreath or garland) to each person. You can make these using florists wire and leaf shapes cut from paper.*
- *Have on hand classical music to play—especially the popular graduation song "Pomp and Circumstance."*

WEB SITE NOTE: *Be sure to check out www.group.com/blockbusterevents for great resources to promote and plan these events!*

The Red Carpet

As teenagers arrive, ask them to don their togas and, if you've provided them, laurel wreaths (see "Bonus Swag"). Ask students to take a seat somewhere in the "classroom." Quietly distribute the six cards from the "Spin Zone" handout to six students, both male and female, who you feel would be able to convince the audience they are speaking the truth even if they're telling a lie.

Once everyone is seated, say:

Welcome to Western Civilization class and the foundation of democracy! I'm glad to see you're all wearing togas, which indicated your profession, social status, and even honor in ancient Rome. By the end of our lesson, you all will see the value of weaving into your lives integrity deserving of the highest honor. While we're waiting for our guest lecturer, Mr. Hundert, let's practice our oratorical skills.

The Spin Zone

Say: **In John 8:32, Jesus says that we will know the truth and it will set us free. We're going to see if we can recognize the truth!**

Ask the six people to whom you handed the "Spin Zone" cards to come to the front. As they make their way forward, say: **We have three pairs of people who will be telling us about themselves. In each pair, one person is telling the truth and the other is lying. Once both people have presented their stories, it will be up to you, the audience, to decide who is telling the truth.**

When everyone understands, have the first person and then the second tell his or her stories. Thank the storytellers; then ask the group to vote on which person was telling the truth. Take a vote, and then ask the person who was telling the truth to step forward. Repeat this process with the next two pairs. Then ask:

- *What kinds of "white lies" do people tell every day?*
- *Do people have to exhibit a high level of integrity to be successful in our society? Why or why not?*
- *What does this tell you about our culture?*

Say: **Our society is filled with people who speak half-truths, practice political spin, and tell outright lies. It's difficult to know whom to trust. That's why we're going to learn more about integrity from our guest speaker, Mr. Hundert. As you listen to his experience, think about your own life and whether your current values would be enough to grant you membership into the Emperor's Club.**

The Production—*The Emperor's Club*

Gather everyone around the TV to watch the movie. Start the film, sit back, relax, and enjoy!

Postproduction

Discussion

Give everyone a five-minute stretch and bathroom break. As your students return, have them form pairs or trios. Ask groups to read Matthew 6:1-6 together and then discuss these questions:

- *What does the word integrity mean to you in light of this passage?*
- *Do you think "little" choices like cheating on tests or showing disrespect to a teacher really make that big of an impact on the direction of a person's life? Why or why not?*
- *What are some of the little compromises you or others have made?*
- *How would the world be different if people chose integrity over compromise?*

Say: **Small choices can make a big impact on character over time. You build a foundation for your character when you're young, and the sturdiness of** that foundation determines the strength of your character when you're older.

How Did I Get Here?

Reveal the large map of the U.S. Say: **Life can look like a cross-country trip where birth is your hometown and death is far, far away on the other side. Hopefully our destination is heaven, where we hope to hear Jesus say, "Well done, my good and faithful servant." Obviously the quickest route between these two points is a straight line. Unfortunately many people indulge in detours that can get them way off track. Jesus presents a picture of very different outcomes at the end of life in Matthew 25:14-30.**

Read this passage from *The Message* or the New Living Translation. Then point out the two towns you've highlighted on the map. Explain that each person will take a turn throwing a dart to try to hit the destination; then you'll draw a straight line from your town to the dart.

Have students line up and take turns throwing the dart. Use the yardstick and marker to draw a straight line between your town and the place that each person's dart lands. When everyone has had a turn, say: **Even the smallest deviation has the potential to lead you off the path of righteousness over a lifetime. Thankfully, God gives us detailed instructions for avoiding those mistakes.**

Have teenagers form trios or quartets and read Proverbs 4 with their groups. Then ask them to discuss the following questions:

- *Why don't people pursue or listen to wisdom?*
- *What are some methods for acquiring this type of wisdom?*
- *How can you remind yourself to act upon the wisdom you acquire?*
- *How could someone get back on the path of wisdom after a diversion?*

Following the Path

Gather everyone together around the sheet of newsprint you taped up. Say: **Mr. Hundert pointed out that one of the best ways to stay on course is to "follow** the path where great men have walked." That phrase echoes what the Bible teaches as well.

Have volunteers read aloud 2 Thessalonians 3:3-9 and Hebrews 12:1-3. Then encourage teenagers to suggest names of people from the Bible, from history, and from their personal lives who provide examples worth following. Write "Jesus" at the top of the sheet of newsprint, and then ask students for their recommendations. Write a dozen or so suggested names—both male and female—and ask teenagers to explain why they recommend those individuals.

Say: **This is a great list of people from whom we all can learn. You have the opportunity to set your feet to walk on the path of integrity that the heroes of faith have set before us. One way to help you do so is by looking ahead to the end of life. Knowing where you want to end up will help you make the correct decisions along the path.**

Distribute a "Following the Path" handout (p. 23) and pens or pencils to each participant.
Point out the box titled "epitaph" at the top of the page.

Say: **An epitaph is a short statement written on a person's gravestone to capture what that person meant to family, friends, and the world. These aren't statements about fame or fortune, but are about character. Deciding now what you'd like your gravestone to read will help you make decisions that reflect the kind of person you want to be. This isn't supposed to be a morbid activity. Think about the type of character you hope to demonstrate, perhaps reflecting upon the lives of the people listed on the newsprint for ideas, and write your own epitaph.**

Give everyone plenty of time to work. Then ask for

PRODUCTION TIP

If you strongly disagree with a suggested name, discuss with the group which of that person's characteristics might be worth following and which characteristics may divert someone from the intended path.

SPECIAL EFFECTS

Play a classical music CD, especially one that includes the song "Pomp and Circumstance," while teenagers work.

---

volunteers to share what they wrote, saying: **By sharing our epitaphs, we can help support one another in working toward our goals.**

After volunteers share, explain that the next step is to think about how to live every day in a way that leads toward those character goals. Say: **Others have faced difficult decisions and temptations, just as you do and will, and they've chosen the path of integrity.**

Have teenagers each choose someone from the people included on the newsprint list—someone they admire and want to emulate. Say: **On your handouts, the person figure represents who you are today, right now. The epitaph, as we discussed, represents your character goals. What can you learn from the person you chose about how to grow in character? What actions did he or she take? What choices did that person make? What lifestyle decisions did they make? In the spaces provided, write five things that will help you follow the path to your goal.**

After teenagers have finished, remind them that the actions they listed are not to be interpreted as a method of earning God's love and grace since God loves them now and always, no matter what. Instead, living a life of integrity is a way to honor, glorify, thank, and introduce others to God. Say: **When you face even small decisions, remember that others who have come before you faced similar choices. Some, represented by Sedgewick, made choices that led them off course. Others laid down a path that you can follow to your goal.**

SPECIAL EFFECTS

To lighten the mood after this activity, show a humorous scene from *The Royal Tenenbaums* (rated R) located at 1:41:15–1:43:30 (DVD chapter 12) where the family reads the silly epitaph about their recently deceased father.

Word of Mouth
Praying the Path

Read aloud Matthew 6:33, and then point out the masking tape path on the floor. Say: **Now follow the path we have laid out for you. As you walk along this path, pray about your response to Matthew 6:33, about the goals you created, and about wisdom.** Give teenagers about 10 minutes to pray as they walk the path, and encourage silence as they do so. Afterward, close the event by praying for God's guidance for students as they go to pursue their character goals.

SPECIAL EFFECTS

Play a classical music CD, especially one that includes the song "Pomp and Circumstance," while teenagers walk and pray.

Suggested Overnight Retreat Schedule

If you'd like to extend this event into an overnight retreat, use this schedule as a starting point.

Day	Time	Activities	Supplies
Friday	7:00 p.m.-7:20 p.m.	*The Spin Zone*	"Spin Zone" handout (p. 22), scissors
	7:20 p.m.-9:10 p.m.	*The Emperor's Club*	Movie: *The Emperor's Club*, DVD player or VCR, TV
	9:10 p.m.-9:30 p.m.	*Discussion*	Bibles
	9:30 p.m.-10:30 p.m.	Toga party	
	10:30 p.m.-11:30 p.m.	Free time	
	Midnight	Lights out	
Saturday	8:00 a.m.-8:30 a.m.	Devotion	
	8:30 a.m.-9:00 a.m.	Breakfast	
	9:00 a.m.-9:30 a.m.	*How Did I Get Here?*	Bibles, mounted U.S. map, easel, dart, marker, yardstick
	9:30 a.m.-noon	Games or group activities	
	Noon-1:00 p.m.	Lunch	
	1:00 p.m.-3:00 p.m.	Free time	
	3:00 p.m.-4:00 p.m.	*Following the Path*	Bible, newsprint, tape, marker, "Following the Path" handouts (p. 23), pens or pencils
		Praying the Path	Bible, masking tape
	4:00 p.m.-5:00 p.m.	Free time	
	5:00 p.m.-6:00 p.m.	Dinner	
	6:00 p.m.-7:30 p.m.	Worship and prayer	
	7:30 p.m.-8:00 p.m.	Pack and leave	

Spin Zone

BOX 1: Create a fake fact about your life, and convince the group that it's true. Make your "fact" as believable as possible so you can fool the group.

BOX 2: Create a fake fact about your life, and convince the group that it's true. Make your "fact" as believable as possible so you can fool the group.

BOX 3: Create a fake fact about your life, and convince the group that it's true. Make your "fact" as believable as possible so you can fool the group.

BOX 4: Tell an interesting fact about yourself that people in the group might not know and might not believe. Do your best to convince the group that it's true.

BOX 5: Tell an interesting fact about yourself that people in the group might not know and might not believe. Do your best to convince the group that it's true.

BOX 6: Tell an interesting fact about yourself that people in the group might not know and might not believe. Do your best to convince the group that it's true.

Following the Path

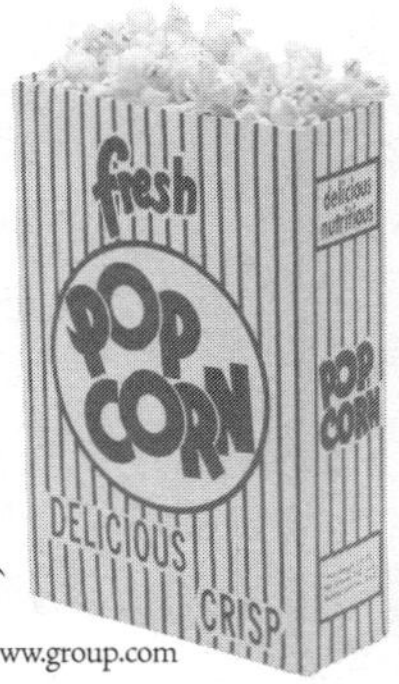

5

EPITAPH

4

3

1

2

Following the Path

fresh
POP
CORN
POP
CORN
DELICIOUS
CRISP

Rating:

G

The Props

- ☐ *Bibles*
- ☐ *movie: Finding Nemo*
- ☐ *DVD player or VCR*
- ☐ *TV or video projector*
- ☐ *frozen whole fish—head and all!*
- ☐ *white butcher paper*
- ☐ *paints or markers*
- ☐ *fish-shaped crackers*
- ☐ *6-foot folding table*
- ☐ *several framed photos of people*
- ☐ *1 scooter*
- ☐ *4 empty, rinsed, one-gallon milk jugs*
- ☐ *glue*
- ☐ *magazines*
- ☐ *one 6-foot 2x4 beam*
- ☐ *3 cinder blocks*
- ☐ *20 one-dollar bills (or play money)*
- ☐ *masking tape*
- ☐ *stack of textbooks*
- ☐ *10- to 20-gallon cooking pot*
- ☐ *wet cooked spaghetti*
- ☐ *plastic fish*
- ☐ *permanent marker*
- ☐ *paper towels*
- ☐ *pens or pencils*
- ☐ *1 "God Loves Me" handout (p. 29) for each person*

Take 24
Blockbuster
Movie Events

Searching for the One:
God's Frantic Love

The Pitch

Finding Nemo depicts a father fish's frantic search for his missing son. His hunt mirrors the attitude God has for each of us, his (sometimes extremely lost) sheep. Students will have a deeper appreciation for and understanding of the incomprehensible depth of love that God has for each of them after experiencing this event.

Favorite Quote

"What do you think? If a man owns a hundred sheep, and one of them wanders away, will he not leave the ninety-nine on the hills and go to look for the one that wandered off? And if he finds it, I tell you the truth, he is happier about that one sheep than about the ninety-nine that did not wander off. In the same way your Father in heaven is not willing that any of these little ones should be lost" (Matthew 18:12-14).

More Quotables: Psalm 23; Luke 15:1-7; Romans 8:38-39

Suggested Schedule

Section	Activities	Time	Supplies
The Red Carpet	*Finding Nemo*	20-25 minutes	Bible, fish, butcher paper, markers or paints, fish-shaped crackers
The Production	*Finding Nemo*	100 minutes	Movie: *Finding Nemo*, DVD player or VCR, TV
Postproduction	*Discussion*	10-15 minutes	Bible
	Getting Carried Away	30-35 minutes	Bibles, folding table, framed pictures, scooter, milk jugs, glue, pictures of media, 2x4 beam, cinder blocks, dollar bills, tape, textbooks
	How Deep Is His Love?	15-20 minutes	Bibles, toy fish, permanent marker, cooking pot, cooked spaghetti, paper towels
Word of Mouth	*God Loves Me*	10-15 minutes	"God Loves Me" handout (p. 29), pens or pencils

Movie Review

Finding Nemo is an animated account of the amazing journey of Marlin, an overprotective clownfish, as he swims across the ocean through treacherous circumstances in order to rescue his only son, Nemo. Marlin faces sharks, jellyfish, and a horde of selfish seagulls with faithful Dory, a fish with short-term memory loss. Marlin learns that his son is growing up and that he has to let go. This film is truly a hilarious and touching tale of a father's love for his son.

We know that God loves us, but it's eye-opening to see the intensity and passion with which God pursues us individually. The Creator of the universe loves us with the kind of love that would face the cross. This event is meant to remind your teenagers that, without a shadow of a doubt, God loves them personally and completely.

Pastoral Guidance

Finding Nemo is clean as a whistle. If you find offense here, you probably don't leave the house—and you definitely shouldn't be using this book. (See page 5 for more details, or visit www.screenit.com or a detailed list of the film's content.)

Preproduction

Set up a movie viewing area with the TV or projector and VCR or DVD player. Have the movie set up and ready to go.

Freeze a fresh fish, head and all, in white butcher paper (the kind the fish is wrapped in if you bought it from your local grocer). Use paints or markers to create a replica of Nemo (an orange, white, and black clownfish) on the white butcher paper. Hide the fish somewhere within the boundaries you'll set for the "Finding Nemo" hunt—somewhere challenging but not impossible.

Create an obstacle course either in your meeting room or nearby. Set up a 6-foot folding table lengthwise for students to crawl under, and place several framed pictures of people on top. Place a scooter at the end of the table. Then place four empty gallon-sized milk jugs for the scooter to weave around. On each side of the milk cartons, glue pictures from magazines that represent different types of media so that racers must weave around movies, music, TV, and video games. Next place a 6-foot 2x4 piece of wood across three cinder blocks as a balance beam. Spread the dollar bills on the floor on both sides of the balance beam. Then use masking tape to create a series of seven vertical boxes on the floor—similar to hopscotch. In the second box, write "sex" on a piece of paper; in the fifth, write "drugs"; in the sixth, write "junk food." Finally, leave a sizable stack of textbooks on the floor at the end of the hopscotch pattern.

Find 14 toy fish (from a local party supply store or from www.orientaltrading.com under "Animal Toys"), and use a permanent marker to write one of these Scripture references on each fish: Genesis 9:8-17; Numbers 14:18-19; Deuteronomy 7:9; Nehemiah 9:6; Psalm 103:17; Psalm 119:103-105; Joel 2:13; Matthew 6:25-33; Matthew 7:7-11; John 3:16-17;

Take 25
Blockbuster Movie Events

John 14:16-18; Romans 5:8; Romans 8:35-39; and 1 John 4:16. Then fill a large metal cooking pot (10 to 20 gallons, if possible) with damp spaghetti (cooked but not dry and sticky). Mix in the toy fish, and stash the cooking pot out of sight (covered so the spaghetti doesn't dry out).

Bonus Swag

Use these ideas to produce even more of the movie's ambience throughout this event.

- *Transform your meeting room into an underwater oasis by draping blue sheets or streamers from the ceiling to the floor. Position fans to blow the sheets like waves along the wall.*
- *Place fish tanks or goldfish bowls around the room, and fill them with live or toy sea creatures.*
- *Find toy underwater creatures such as sharks, fish, crabs, and octopuses to hang from the ceiling or tape to the wall.*
- *Set bowls of fish-shaped crackers around the meeting area.*

WEB SITE NOTE: *Be sure to check out www.group.com/blockbusterevents for great resources to promote and plan these events!*

The Red Carpet
Finding Nemo

Once everyone has arrived, say: **Nemo is lost somewhere in the church, and we need to find him! When you find Nemo, don't rescue him. Your job is to help everyone else find him as well. You have to go back to the [central place] and do a charade that will clue in people to Nemo's location. You can't say a word! Obviously, the more people find Nemo, the more people will be doing charades. Once everyone finds Nemo, rescue the little fish and bring him back here.**

Explain the boundaries in detail, then let teenagers loose!

When everyone returns from finding Nemo, reward everyone with fish-shaped crackers. Then ask:

- ***Has anyone here ever been really lost before? How did that feel?***

Have someone read aloud Luke 15:1-7 to the group.
Ask: • ***Why does God care so much about the one over the 99?***

Say: **We're going to see one father's desperate search for his lost child. As we watch *Finding Nemo*, think about how God loves you with an even greater passion than Marlin shows for Nemo.**

The Production—*Finding Nemo*

Gather everyone around the TV to watch the movie. Start the film, sit back, relax, and enjoy! Try to mooch some fish-shaped crackers.

Postproduction
Discussion

When the movie ends, let everyone stretch or go to the restrooms. After five minutes, gather everyone back together. Have teenagers form groups of two or three, and then ask a volunteer to read aloud Matthew 18:12-14.
Ask: • ***Do you believe God has pursued you as Marlin pursued Nemo? Why or why not?***
- ***Have you ever personally experienced God's love in a tangible way? If so, how?***

Getting Carried Away

Say: **As the Scripture shows, God will go to great lengths to find us. Unfortunately, people sometimes become snagged as Nemo was; something in life drags them off course and prevents them from experiencing God's love.**
Ask: • ***What are some things you've seen "snag" people?***

Say: **You're going to practice avoiding some of the things that can carry a person away from God's love by navigating an obstacle course.**

Have students form two teams. Have the teams stand at either end of the obstacle course. Demonstrate the course as you explain it.

Say: **Our obstacle course represents some things that might carry you away. Friends, peers, or co-workers might lead you off course. Crawl underneath the table without knocking any pictures over. Then you ride the scooter through media influences, which include movies, TV, video games, and music. Next you walk the balance beam without falling to the temptation of materialism. Then hop on one leg over the pitfalls of sex, drugs, or junk food. Finally, you have to deal with intellectualism, which makes people think they are too smart for God's love. Grab the stack of books and walk backward to the finish without dropping a book. Hand the books to the next person in line, who will then complete the obstacle course in the opposite direction.**

SPECIAL EFFECTS

Have fun, upbeat rock or hip-hop music playing while youth complete the obstacle course.

When teenagers understand what to do, start them on the obstacle course.

Once everyone takes a turn running through the obstacle course, have students form groups of three or four. Ask a volunteer in each group to read aloud Romans 8:38-39. Then have groups discuss the following questions:

- *Why doesn't everyone experience God's love if nothing can separate us from it?*
- *What are some ways that God displays love for us?*
- *How can people cling to God's love and protect themselves from getting distracted by something else?*

How Deep Is His Love?

Bring everyone back together.

Say: **God's love is perfect, and we should never accept a cheap substitute. God does everything possible to chase us down and bring us home. God gladly would go to the bottom of the ocean to get us—that's how rich and deep his love is.**

Have teenagers form 14 groups (or groups of three if

you have fewer than 30 students) and gather around the large cooking pot. Have each group select one person to be the group's "deep-sea diver." Have divers stand next to you.

Say: **Each diver will be plunging down deep into the sea, reaching inside a mass of sea anemones, to bring out a fish. You'll take the fish back to your group. A verse is written on the fish. In your group, you'll read the verse and discuss what it says about God's love.**

Allow divers to search for the fish, and provide paper towels for drying their hands afterward. Then have groups discuss the verses. After several minutes of discussion, bring everyone back together.

Ask:
- *What did you learn about God's love from your Scripture?*
- *How does God demonstrate love for us?*
- *How would you describe God's love for us in your own words?*

Say: **Even though God has done a lot to show us love, many people still don't believe that God's love is everything it's cracked up to be.**
- *If God is love, why does he punish people?*
- *How can a loving God possibly allow bad things to happen to good people?*
- *Can anyone possibly have assurance that God truly loves him or her? Why or why not?*

Say: **These are some common questions, but hopefully you've seen and learned tonight that God answers them in the best way possible—by reaching out to everyone personally with the promise of perfect, unconditional love.**

Word of Mouth
God Loves Me

Distribute a copy of the "God Loves Me" handout (p. 29) and a pen or pencil to each person.

Say: God loves each and every one of you dearly. I know that's hard to believe or feel sometimes since we don't feel physical hugs or audible affirmation. God demonstrates love in many other ways, though—through the beautiful creation, the gift of salvation, a connection in prayer, and through his love letter to the world, the Holy Bible.

We're going to make one chapter from this love letter a little more personal right now. Psalm 23, one of the most quoted psalms in Scripture, was written with you in mind. To help you see that, you're simply going to substitute your name for the pronouns.

Once you've finished filling in the blanks with your name, read the poem silently to yourself, soaking in the promises that God is giving you. You might even want to spend some time in prayer, thanking God for his love. Take this time to hang out with the God who loves you.

SPECIAL EFFECTS
Play some mellow worship music while students write and pray.

Suggested Overnight Retreat Schedule

If you'd like to extend this event into an overnight retreat, use this schedule as a starting point.

Day	Time	Activities	Supplies
Friday	7:00 p.m.-7:25 p.m.	*Finding Nemo*	Bible, fish, butcher paper, markers or paints, fish-shaped crackers
	7:25 p.m.-9:05 p.m.	*Finding Nemo*	Movie: *Finding Nemo*, DVD player or VCR, TV
	9:05 p.m.-9:20 p.m.	*Discussion*	Bible
	9:20 p.m.-10:00 p.m.	Snacks	
	10:00 p.m.-11:30 p.m.	Free time	
	Midnight	Lights out	
Saturday	8:00 a.m.-8:30 a.m.	Devotion	
	8:30 a.m.-9:00 a.m.	Breakfast	
	9:00 a.m.-9:35 a.m.	*Getting Carried Away*	Bibles, folding table, framed pictures, scooter, milk jugs, glue, pictures of media, 2x4 beam, cinder blocks, dollar bills, tape, textbooks
	9:35 a.m.-noon	Games or group activities	
	Noon-1:00 p.m.	Lunch	
	1:00 p.m.-3:00 p.m.	Free time	
	3:00 p.m.-3:35 p.m.	*How Deep Is His Love?*	Bibles, toy fish, permanent marker, cooking pot, cooked spaghetti, paper towels
		God Loves Me	"God Loves Me" handout (p. 29), pens or pencils
	3:35 p.m.-5:00 p.m.	Free time	
	5:00 p.m.-6:00 p.m.	Dinner	
	6:00 p.m.-7:30 p.m.	Worship and prayer	
	7:30 p.m.-8:00 p.m.	Pack and leave	

God Loves Me

PSALM 23

THE LORD IS   SHEPHERD, I SHALL NOT BE IN WANT. HE
MAKES   LIE DOWN IN GREEN PASTURES, HE LEADS
          BESIDE QUIET WATERS, HE RESTORES   SOUL.
HE GUIDES   IN PATHS OF RIGHTEOUSNESS FOR HIS NAME'S
SAKE. EVEN THOUGH   WALKS THROUGH THE VALLEY OF
THE SHADOW OF DEATH,   WILL FEAR NO EVIL, FOR YOU ARE
WITH   ; YOUR ROD AND YOUR STAFF, THEY COMFORT
. YOU PREPARE A TABLE BEFORE   IN THE
PRESENCE OF   ENEMIES. YOU ANOINT   HEAD
WITH OIL;   CUP OVERFLOWS. SURELY GOODNESS AND LOVE
WILL FOLLOW   ALL THE DAYS OF   LIFE, AND
          WILL DWELL IN THE HOUSE OF THE LORD FOREVER.

God Loves Me

Rating:

PG for mild thematic elements and some language

The Props

☐ *Bibles*
☐ *movie:* Freaky Friday
☐ *DVD player or VCR*
☐ *TV or video projector*
☐ *takeout boxes from a Chinese restaurant (These often can be purchased from craft stores, too.)*
☐ *popcorn*
☐ *dress clothes for teenagers to dress up in—such as ties, coats, dresses, slacks, dress shirts, pantyhose, and heels*
☐ *paper*
☐ *pens or pencils*
☐ *fortune cookies (See Preproduction, page 31, for details.)*

Take a Walk in My Shoes:
Finding Compassion for Others

The Pitch

Freaky Friday uses the hilarious premise of a mother and daughter switching bodies to show what it's like to walk in someone else's shoes. Students who experience this event will gain new insight into seeking other perspectives, having the compassion of Christ for other people, and discovering how doing so reflects the kingdom of God.

Favorite Quote

"Be kind and compassionate to one another, forgiving each other, just as in Christ God forgave you" (Ephesians 4:32).

More Quotables: Matthew 7:3-5; Romans 12:15-16; 2 Corinthians 1:3-7

Suggested Schedule

Section	Activities	Time	Supplies
The Red Carpet	*Imitation Is a Sincere Form*	15-20 minutes	
The Production	*Freaky Friday*	105 minutes	Movie: *Freaky Friday*, DVD player or VCR, TV, popcorn, Chinese takeout boxes
Postproduction	*Discussion*	10-15 minutes	Bible
	A New Skin	25-30 minutes	Bibles, dress clothes
	Flip the Compassion Switch	25-30 minutes	Bibles, paper, pens or pencils
Word of Mouth	*A Fortune in Compassion*	5-10 minutes	Fortune cookies

Movie Review

Anna Coleman (Lindsay Lohan) and her mother, Tess (Jamie Lee Curtis), are on each other's last nerve. The conflict rages at revolutionary proportions as Tess' marriage to Ryan (Mark Harmon) approaches. Anna insists that her mother wants to ruin her life, and Tess believes her daughter is utterly selfish and self-absorbed. Both receive a rude awakening when a fortune cookie magically causes them to switch bodies, with the only hope of reversal in learning the meaning of selfless love. Tess, as Anna, must navigate the high school halls—which is much more treacherous than she knew. Likewise Anna, as Tess, must counsel her mother's patients, learning a thing or two about her mother's life and the weight of responsibility. While completely messing up one another's lives, the Colemans come to understand and love one another more deeply than they ever could have while residing inside their own skins.

How does one break out of a self-centered worldview and look with compassion on the lives of others? *Freaky Friday* answers this problem in a way that's impossible to mimic but that opens the hearts and minds of viewers. While Jesus makes it clear that we are to serve the "least of these," judge not without facing judgment ourselves, and seek ways to lay down our lives, these attitudes don't come hard-wired into humanity's genetic code. Even when the influence of the Holy Spirit activates our atrophied compassion cells, we seem to respond to family members last. Whether it's that familiarity breeds contempt or that we simply don't perceive our family members as needing compassion, this event will convince your young people that a ministry of compassion begins at home.

Pastoral Guidance

Freaky Friday is almost devoid of offensive material, though it makes extensive use of the words "suck" and "God" as substitutes for curse words. There's also a brief shot of the top of Jamie Lee Curtis' thong underwear played for comedic effect. Finally, some might object to the whole concept of two people switching bodies. Explain to your teenagers that the film is a fairy tale about compassion. The body switch is not the point of the film but is merely a fantastical device for setting a moral story in motion. (See page 5 for more details or visit www.screenit.com for a detailed list of the film's content.)

Preproduction

Set up a movie viewing area with the TV or projector and DVD player or VCR. Have the movie set up and ready to go.

Fill the Chinese takeout boxes with popcorn as a movie snack.

Gather dress clothes that participants can put on over their clothing—ties, coats, dresses, slacks, dress shirts, high-heeled shoes, and anything else you can beg or borrow, or buy from secondhand stores. Place these in a pile in an easily accessible location that you can cover or hide until the proper time.

Provide "fortune cookies" with Ephesians 4:32 written out as the fortune. For crème

de la crème fortune cookies, do an Internet search and find where you can purchase real fortune cookies with custom fortunes. For those on a more limited budget, buy cookies (without crème filling) at your local grocery store. Print the verse on strips of paper, cut apart the strips, roll them up, and stick them inside the cookies. For a totally low-budget yet unforgettable fortune cookie, simply buy some crème-filled sandwich cookies. Separate the cookie from the filling, lay the strip of paper with the verse printed on it across the filling, and put the cookie back together. (Yes, the fortune will stick out on either side. It's so bad that it's funny!)

Bonus Swag

Use these ideas to produce even more of the movie's ambience throughout this event.

- *Give your room a split-personality makeover. Turn one side into a stereotypical teen's bedroom, complete with piles of clothes on the floor, movie star and rock band posters on the walls, and a bed with sheets looking like they ended up on the wrong side of a fight with a tornado. Allow the sterile hand of a parent to commandeer the other side of the room, complete with a lame painting of flowers or the countryside over a showroom-style bed and a straight-laced business suit carefully draped over a straight-backed chair.*
- *Have on hand a CD player and the* Freaky Friday *soundtrack on CD.*

SPECIAL EFFECTS

Invite parents and their teenagers to attend this event together. Both generations not only will enjoy the film, but also will learn about one another.

As a side benefit, the parents will be exposed to the youth ministry and will experience the exciting, innovative ways you're connecting their teenagers' everyday lives to a transforming faith!

WEB SITE NOTE: *Be sure to check out www.group.com/blockbusterevents for great resources to promote and plan these events!*

The Red Carpet
Imitation Is a Sincere Form

Greet participants as they arrive, and have them form groups of four. After everyone has arrived and has found a group, say: **Each one of you has a very simple assignment: Just as the actors on** *Saturday Night Live* **perform impersonations of the president or celebrities, you'll perform an impression of one of your parents. Specifically, you'll imitate how you believe your parents view you when you leave the house to go out with your friends. What do you think they say about you once you're out of the room? For those of you who aren't quite clear on what I mean, please enjoy my impersonation of my** [mother/father] **talking about me as a teen.** Spend a moment imitating the parent of your choice.

Instruct groups to share their impersonations, starting with the oldest person in each group. Wander among the groups, encouraging students in their portrayals.

When participants have shared their impressions, allow volunteers to share their impersonations with the

SPECIAL EFFECTS

Have the *Freaky Friday* movie soundtrack playing as participants arrive.

SPECIAL EFFECTS

If adults are in attendance, have them break into groups to perform imitations of their children in the same way— what they imagine that their teenagers say about them once they leave the house with their friends.

PRODUCTION TIP

The purpose of this activity obviously is not for adults and teenagers to hurt one another's feelings or express their anger and frustration. You know your teenagers and their parents; set the proper stage for this activity so that participants can have fun and learn about each other rather than hurt each other.

whole group.

Afterward, say: **Tonight is a very special night. Not only are we going to enjoy a wonderful movie, but we also are going to learn more about ourselves, our relationships with others, and compassion. Paul commands us in Ephesians 4:32 to "be kind and compassionate to one another, forgiving each other, just as in Christ God forgave you." Think about that verse as you watch the crazy events of** *Freaky Friday*!

The Production — *Freaky Friday*

Gather everyone around the TV to watch the movie. Set out Chinese takeout boxes full of popcorn, start the film, sit back, relax, and enjoy!

Postproduction

Discussion

When the movie ends, allow a five-minute stretch and bathroom break. When everyone returns, ask participants to form groups of three or four to discuss the following questions:

- *Why was it so difficult for Anna and Tess to be compassionate toward one another? Do you relate? Why or why not?*
- *Do you think it's more difficult to be compassionate toward your own family members than toward strangers or friends? Why or why not?*
- *What hurdles prevent you from showing compassion to others?*

Say: **It can be difficult not to view other people and situations through the filter of "What can they do for me?" Tonight, though, we're going to get "freaky" and try to change our view so we're looking through the filter of "What's life like for other people, and how can I help them?"**

Ask a volunteer to read aloud Matthew 7:3-5. Then ask:

- *How do you feel when someone tries to take a speck out of your eye?*
- *Why do you try to take the specks out of other people's eyes?*

Say: **To really live out these verses, we all need to endure a radical transformation.**

A New Skin

You've probably heard the phrase "Walk a mile in my shoes." Ask teenagers for their ideas about what the saying means.

Say: **Basically, people shouldn't judge until they've been through the same experiences. God gave us an amazing gift: Even though we can't physically live another person's life as Anna and Tess did for a day, we can use our imagination to picture what life is like for another person. Unfortunately, we don't always use this gift of empathy. Let's practice empathy by putting on "new skin."**

Reveal the dress clothes you collected. Say: **We're going to break in a second. When we do, first read Romans 12:15-16 to yourself silently. While thinking about** how those verses relate to compassion, get something to wear from this pile of clothes. You can put on as many pieces of clothing as you want, but everyone should have at least one piece of clothing. Take a few minutes to review the verses and put on your new skin.

Once everyone has at least one piece of new clothing on, have students form groups of four to six. Say: **Let's really slip into the skin of someone new, trying to understand what it's like to walk in someone else's shoes.** Have groups discuss these questions:

- *How does it feel to wear clothes that aren't your own?*
- *In what ways does this compare with having compassion for others?*
- *Do you find it easy to have compassion for others? Why or why not?*

- *What attitudes or beliefs make it difficult for you to understand the emotions and perspectives of another person?*
- *How can you walk in someone else's shoes without physically playing "dress-up"?*
- *How would making habits from those actions affect your relationships with others?*

After several minutes, have everyone join together again and share ideas from the discussions.

Flip the Compassion Switch

Distribute a sheet of paper and a pen or pencil to each person. Say: **We're going to put your ideas to the test by "switching places" with someone and trying to find compassion for him or her. Close your eyes and think of a person that you don't get along with. It could be someone you're fighting with, someone you simply don't like, or even someone you don't know such as a person from a group of whom you're wary. When you've thought of someone, open your eyes.**

When all eyes are open, say: **Close your eyes again. Now imagine that you're trapped inside that person's body for a day. What challenges do you face? What are your hopes and dreams? What motivates you to get up in the morning? What causes you anxiety or fear?**

Pause for several minutes. Then say: **You can open your eyes now. Take the next 15 minutes to compose a poem about that person's life. You can write about beliefs, experiences, fears— anything. This is a time**

to frame this person as a uniquely created and beloved child of God.

As everyone works, indicate several times how much time is left. Afterward, ask for volunteers to share their poems with the group without indicating whom the poem is about. Allow those who have stage fright to have someone else read their poems. Afterward, have participants form the same groups from the previous activity to discuss these questions:

- *How did it feel to think intentionally about someone else's life?*
- *What's the point of trying to develop compassion for others?*
- *What other ways can you develop compassion?*

Have groups read 2 Corinthians 1:3-7 and then discuss these questions:

- *What is God's purpose for compassion?*
- *When people show you compassion, how are you affected?*
- *How are you affected when you show compassion to others?*

Word of Mouth
A Fortune in Compassion

Distribute a fortune cookie to each person. Say: **Having compassion for others often isn't easy. Most of us like to receive compassion, but we tend to forget to extend it to others. Expressing empathy for every person you meet exemplifies the love of Christ in a powerful way. We must be willing to walk in other people's shoes just as Jesus did all the way to the cross.**

Instruct participants to read the fortune, then close their eyes and eat the cookie. Say: **Chew slowly and let the cookie dissolve in your mouth. As you eat, pray that God will help you to see others the way Jesus does—with a love and compassion that passes all understanding. Ask God for opportunities to show compassion this week and for the wisdom and courage to act.**

Close the event by praying that God would inspire Christ's compassion for others within each participant.

Suggested Overnight Retreat Schedule

If you'd like to extend this event into an overnight retreat, use this schedule as a starting point.

Day	Time	Activities	Supplies
Friday	7:00 p.m.-7:20 p.m.	*Imitation Is a Sincere Form*	
	7:20 p.m.-9:05 p.m.	*Freaky Friday*	Movie: *Freaky Friday*, DVD player or VCR, TV, popcorn, Chinese takeout boxes
	9:05 p.m.-9:20 p.m.	*Discussion*	Bible
	9:20 p.m.-9:45 p.m.	Snacks	
	9:45 p.m.-10:15 p.m.	Write thank-you letters to parents.	
	10:15 p.m.-11:30 p.m.	Free time	
	Midnight	Lights out	
Saturday	8:00 a.m.-8:30 a.m.	Devotion	
	8:30 a.m.-9:00 a.m.	Breakfast	
	9:00 a.m.-10:00 a.m.	*A New Skin*	Bibles, dress clothes
		Flip the Compassion Switch	Bibles, paper, pens or pencils
	10:00 a.m.-noon	Games or group activities	
	Noon-1:00 p.m.	Lunch	
	1:00 p.m.-3:00 p.m.	Free time	
	3:00 p.m.-4:00 p.m.	Compassionate Ministry—Brainstorm practical ideas for making your ministries more compassionate toward parents, visitors, the less fortunate, and so on. Say a little prayer.	
	4:00 p.m.-5:00 p.m.	Free time	
	5:00 p.m.-6:00 p.m.	Dinner	
	6:00 p.m.-7:30 p.m.	Worship and prayer *A Fortune in Compassion*	Fortune cookies
	7:30 p.m.-8:00 p.m.	Pack and leave	

The Props

- ☐ *Bibles*
- ☐ *movie:* Holes
- ☐ *DVD player or VCR*
- ☐ *TV or video projector*
- ☐ *1 self-adhesive name tag for each person*
- ☐ *markers*
- ☐ *large, black plastic trash bag*
- ☐ *scissors*
- ☐ *1 "Treasure Chest Pieces" handout (p. 41)*
- ☐ *1 "Treasure Map" handout (p. 42)*
- ☐ *1 index-card file box*
- ☐ *tape*
- ☐ *"treasure" such as candy, gum, coupons, or gift certificates*
- ☐ *1 self-adhesive note for each person*
- ☐ *pens or pencils*
- ☐ *1 foam cup for each person*
- ☐ *1 plastic spoon for each person*
- ☐ *potting soil*

Digging for Answers:
Why Bad Things Happen to Good People

The Pitch

Watching *Holes* will help your young people explore the popular postmodern question that some use to deny God's existence: Why do bad things happen to good people? Through the film and the event, your students can realize that despite the many reasons bad things happen, people can trust God to create something good from even the most tragic situation.

Favorite Quote

"And we know that in all things God works for the good of those who love him, who have been called according to his purpose" (Romans 8:28).

More Quotables: Genesis 3:14-19; 4:3-8; Psalm 71:1-5; John 9:1-3; Romans 3:9-10; 5:1-5; 8:28; 2 Corinthians 1:3-7

Suggested Schedule

Section	Activities	Time	Supplies
The Red Carpet	*The Hole Truth*	10-15 minutes	Self-adhesive name tags, markers, black trash bag, scissors
The Production	*Holes*	105 minutes	Movie: *Holes*, DVD player or VCR, TV
Postproduction	*Discussion*	10-15 minutes	
	God, the Bad, and Me	35-40 minutes	Bibles, "Treasure Chest Pieces" handout (p. 41), scissors, tape, "Treasure Map" handout (p. 42), "treasure," index-card file box
	The Biblical Enquirer	15-20 minutes	Bibles
Word of Mouth	*Peaceful, Digging Feeling*	10-15 minutes	Self-adhesive notes, pens or pencils, foam cups, spoons, potting soil

Movie Review

Holes introduces Stanley Yelnats (Shia LaBeouf), a young man who follows in his family's tradition of having incredibly bad luck. Wrongfully convicted of stealing a pair of shoes and sentenced to juvenile detention, Stanley joins the ranks of the orange jump-suited teen prisoners at Camp Green Lake. Located in a barren desert wasteland, the "camp" forces the juveniles to dig massive holes as "rehabilitation." As Stanley slowly makes friends among the delinquents, he begins to suspect that the warden (Sigourney Weaver), psychotic guard Mr. Sir (Jon Voight), and whacked-out Dr. Pendanski (Tim Blake Nelson) are less interested in rehabilitation than in finding something buried in the dried-up lake bed. It's up to Stanley and his buddy Zero (Khleo Thomas) to unravel the mystery of the hidden treasure of ancient outlaw Kissing Kate Barlow and use what they discover to secure their freedom.

This movie hits perfect notes of humor, adventure, mystery, sweetness, and meaning; the plot dives into issues such as generational sin, judgment, mercy, racism, friendship, substitution, grace, and oppression. *Holes* becomes a valuable ministry tool by addressing the conundrum of bad things happening to good people. Through this event, your young people will lay the blame for tragedy at the feet of the proper culprits instead of in front of their loving Lord.

Pastoral Guidance

In typical Disney fashion, *Holes* contains a handful of scattered questionable words and a few potentially eyebrow-raising scenes—a shot of Stanley in his underwear when he first arrives at camp, several murders, and a teenager assaulting an adult with a shovel (with no real consequences). A major plot point, however, centers on the "curse" a fortuneteller places upon the Yelnats family. While the occultist overtones might cause concern, you can't skip the scene without completely confusing the story. Instead, point out that seemingly harmless activities such as fortunetelling, palm reading, and horoscopes can have tangible spiritual effects and should be shunned completely. (See page 5 for more details or visit www .screenit.com for a detailed list of the film's content.)

Preproduction

Set up a movie viewing area with the TV or projector and VCR or DVD player. Have the movie set up and ready to go.

Set up a "processing center" in front of your building or meeting room to "book" each participant into "prison." A simple processing center can be composed of a table with markers and self-adhesive name tags on it. Ask an adult volunteer to work the table, and explain what he or she is to do. (See page 38, the Red Carpet, for instructions.) Write out strings of numbers on the self-adhesive name tags. The numbers will look like those given to inmates for their mug

shots. Use the following six-number strings, which participants will later use to form groups: 37402, 48513, 59624, 60735, 71846, 82957.

Cut the seams of a black trash bag to create a black square. Then cut a large circle out of the trash bag square.

Photocopy the "Treasure Chest Pieces" handout (p. 41), cut out the pieces, color them if you want, and tape the pieces to the sides of a standard index-card file box. Then photocopy the "Treasure Map" handout (p. 42), and cut it into six pieces as indicated. Place the pieces in the box, and then fill the box with "treasure"—such as gum, coupons for soft drinks or pizza, movie passes, and candy. Finally, hide the "treasure chest" where it won't be discovered accidentally but where it isn't so difficult to find that your students will need GPS to locate it.

For each participant, fill a foam or plastic cup with potting soil. Place the plastic spoons with the cups.

Bonus Swag

Use these ideas to produce even more of the movie's ambience throughout this event.

- *Create a "Camp Green Lake" banner from newsprint to hang over the entrance to your meeting area.*
- *Post two adult "guards" with matching baseball caps, mirrored sunglasses, and toy guns in front of the meeting area entrance.*
- *Serve onion rings and peach preserves on bread or crackers for snacks, and give everyone a jug of water to drink.*
- *Place stuffed or plastic snakes and lizards around the meeting area.*

WEB SITE NOTE: *Be sure to check out www.group.com/blockbusterevents for great resources to promote and plan these events!*

The Red Carpet

As teenagers arrive, "book" them into "prison." Hand each person a name tag to place in the center of his or her chest. Once students apply the name tags, instruct each person to create a nickname to use while in the "joint." If students can't think of nicknames, allow them to use the names of the film's characters—such as X-Ray,

> **SPECIAL EFFECTS**
>
> While your "prisoners" enter, play the peppy *Holes* movie soundtrack.

Zero, Armpit, Zigzag, Caveman, Magnet, and Twitch. Don't allow students to enter the meeting area; instead have them line up and wait for everyone to arrive.

Once everyone is booked, say: **Welcome to Camp Green Lake! Get the line** *straight,* **and** *be quiet!* **Once inside, find a seat and remain** *silent.* **I know this is supposed to be a fun movie event, but anyone causing problems gets tossed in solitary confinement. Now move in!**

The Hole Truth

Once everyone is inside and seated (with handcuffs removed, if you used them), ask two volunteers to join you at the front to act out a skit. Ask which one of them would like to dig a hole, and hand that person the black trash bag "hole" you prepared. Lead the second volunteer to the other side of the area. Explain that the volunteers are to act out what you say.

Say: **One day under the hot, hot sun,** [first volunteer] **dug a hole.** Allow the first volunteer to "dig" and then place the trash bag "hole" on the floor. **After digging the hole,** [first volunteer] **went back to** [his or her] **seat while the audience clapped.** Allow the volunteer to sit down and the audience to clap. **Later that day,** [second volunteer] **was walking along.** [He or she] **was looking at the trees and birds and didn't notice the hole.** [Second volunteer] **fell into the hole and was badly injured.** Urge your volunteer to writhe in pain for as long as it's funny. [He or she] **screamed, "Why,**

> **SPECIAL EFFECTS**
>
> At the processing center, place each "inmate" in "handcuffs," which you may construct from either flagging tape or cut orange construction fencing (both can be purchased at hardware stores). Instruct inmates to hold out their hands, and then put the tape or plastic rings around their wrists. (Let inmates know they won't be handcuffed for long.)

God? Why did you do this to me?" Thank you, [second volunteer]! **You may return to your seat!**

Lead the audience in clapping again, then say: **I know this was a silly skit, but I want to ask you something.**

- *What's your response when something bad happens to you?*
- *What do you see as God's role, if any, in human misfortune?*

Say: **We're going to explore why bad things happen to good people. Be thinking about that as you watch the movie** *Holes.*

The Production—*Holes*

Gather everyone around the TV to watch the movie. Start the film, sit back, relax, and enjoy!

Postproduction

Discussion

After the movie, allow a five-minute stretch and bathroom break. When everyone has returned, ask:

- *How would you have felt if you'd been one of the characters in the movie who didn't "earn" the bad things that happened to him?*
- *How have you felt when you've been involved in a bad experience that you didn't really deserve?*
- *What do you think about God when you learn of horrible current or historical events that affect seemingly decent people? Explain.*
- *When you hear people blame God for painful or unjust events, do you think it's fair? Why or why not?*

God, the Bad, and Me

Have teenagers form six groups by finding prisoners with identical name tag numbers. Then say: **Let's find out why bad things happen to good people. I've hidden a chest similar to the one Stanley found. The chest contains treasure and the answer to why bad things happen to good people. Find the chest, and bring it to me. After I open the chest, the person who found it will share the treasure with his or her team.**

Explain to your students the boundaries of the treasure hunt and any special rules you wish to include. Then allow students to search.

When someone recovers the treasure chest, show everyone its contents. Hand each group one of the six pieces of the "Treasure Map" handout (p. 42), and say: **The answer to why bad things happen to good people lies within the pieces of this treasure map. Don't worry about the listed Bible character right now; instead, read the first Scripture passage with your group.**

the "Treasure Map" handout (p. 42)

After giving groups a moment to read Scripture, have them discuss the following questions:

- *What do these verses indicate could be sources of tragedy?*
- *Have you ever experienced this? If so, how?*
- *Why doesn't God prevent these things from happening?*

When groups have finished, bring them back together into one large group.

Ask:
- *What did you discover as possible sources for bad things happening to good people?*
- *What reasons might God have for not preventing these things?*

SPECIAL EFFECTS

While your prisoners hunt for treasure, play the peppy *Holes* movie soundtrack.

The Biblical Enquirer

Say: **Now we're going to see how real people experienced the effects of those sources of bad things.**

Have teenagers form their six groups again. Direct them to read about the lives of the Bible characters written on their "treasure map" pieces. After they've had time to read, have them discuss the following questions in their groups:

- *What caused the person's "bad luck"?*
- *If this happened today, how would a tabloid newspaper write the headline about it?*

Ask groups to share with the large group a brief synopsis of their Bible characters' story and the tabloid headline they created. Then ask a volunteer to read aloud Romans 8:28. Ask:

- *How did God use the terrible situation you read about for good?*

Have groups read Romans 5:1-5, and then ask:

- *What hope do these verses give people who are enduring tough times?*
- *What are practical ways for you to cling to God during tough times?*

• *How can you help someone going through hard times without sounding "churchy"?*

Call everyone back together again, and ask groups to share what they discussed.

Word of Mouth
Peaceful, Digging Feeling

Distribute a pen or pencil and a blank self-adhesive note to each person. Say: **Bad things happen to all of us, and we might not understand why. If you're facing something difficult in your life, write it on the sticky note.**

After a minute, direct teenagers to the area where you placed the cups of potting soil. Say: **Take that note over to the cups filled with dirt, and dig a hole with a spoon. As you dig, pray for God's peace and understanding about the situation you wrote down. As you cover the note with dirt, ask God to create something good—something that brings God glory—from that bad situation.** Give participants time to complete the activity. Then close in prayer, asking for God to comfort and strengthen those who face trials.

Suggested Overnight Retreat Schedule

If you'd like to extend this event into an overnight retreat, use this schedule as a starting point.

Day	Time	Activities	Supplies
Friday	7:00 p.m.-7:15 p.m.	*The Hole Truth*	Self-adhesive name tags, markers, black trash bag, scissors
	7:15 p.m.-9:00 p.m.	*Holes*	Movie: *Holes*, DVD player or VCR, TV
	9:00 p.m.-9:15 p.m.	*Discussion*	
	9:15 p.m.-10:00 p.m.	Snacks	
	10:00 p.m.-11:30 p.m.	Free time	
	Midnight	Lights out	
Saturday	8:00 a.m.-8:30 a.m.	Devotion	
	8:30 a.m.-9:00 a.m.	Breakfast	
	9:00 a.m.-10:00 a.m.	*God, the Bad, and Me*	Bibles, "Treasure Chest Pieces" handout (p. 41), scissors, tape, "Treasure Map" handout (p. 42), "treasure," index-card file box
		The Biblical Enquirer	Bibles
	10:00 a.m.-noon	Games or group activities	
	Noon-1:00 p.m.	Lunch	
	1:00 p.m.-3:00 p.m.	Free time	
	3:00 p.m.-3:15 p.m.	*Peaceful, Digging Feeling*	Self-adhesive notes, pens or pencils, foam cups, spoons, potting soil
	3:15 p.m.-5:00 p.m.	Free time	
	5:00 p.m.-6:00 p.m.	Dinner	
	6:00 p.m.-7:30 p.m.	Worship and prayer	
	7:30 p.m.-8:00 p.m.	Pack and leave	

Treasure Chest Pieces

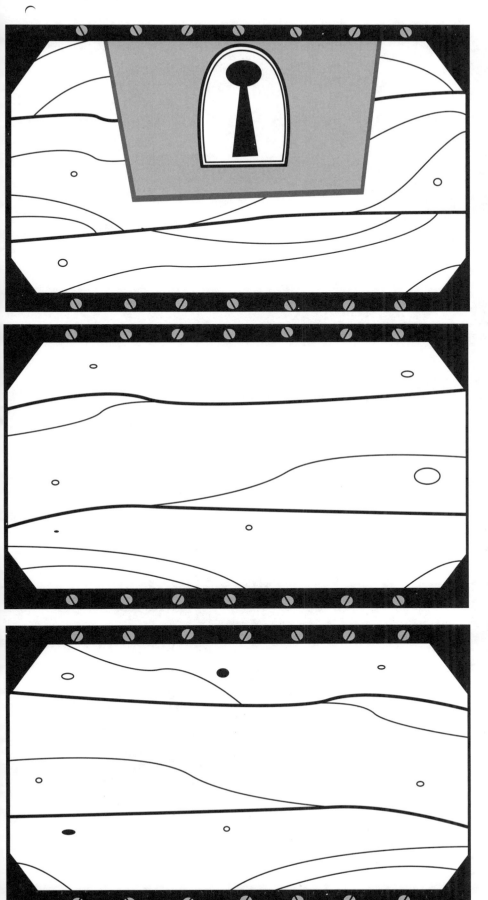

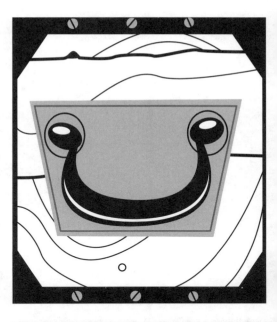

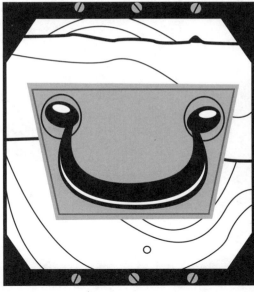

Treasure Map

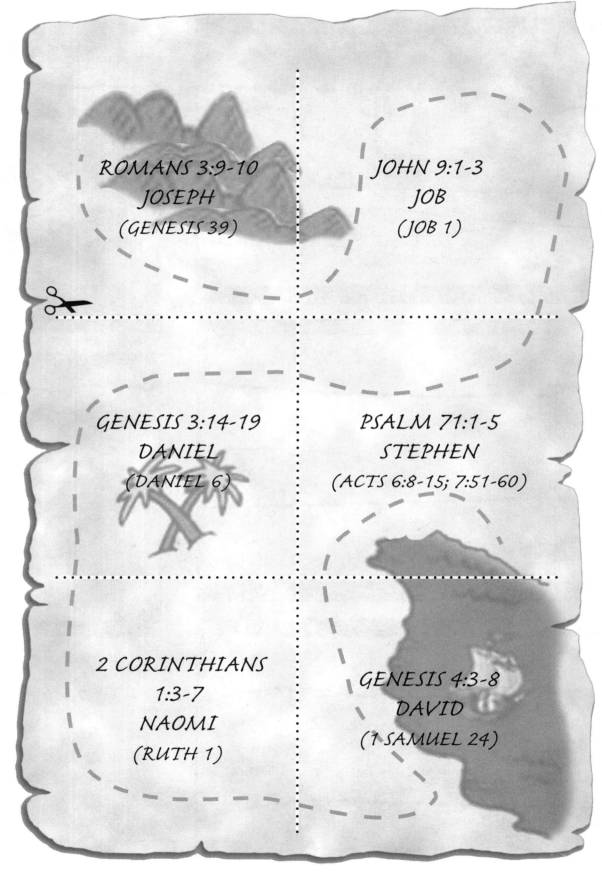

ROMANS 3:9-10
JOSEPH
(GENESIS 39)

JOHN 9:1-3
JOB
(JOB 1)

GENESIS 3:14-19
DANIEL
(DANIEL 6)

PSALM 71:1-5
STEPHEN
(ACTS 6:8-15; 7:51-60)

2 CORINTHIANS
1:3-7
NAOMI
(RUTH 1)

GENESIS 4:3-8
DAVID
(1 SAMUEL 24)

Movie:

Joshua
(Crusader, 2002)

Rating:
G

The Props

- [ ] *Bibles*
- [ ] *movie:* Joshua
- [ ] *DVD player or VCR*
- [ ] *TV or video projector*
- [ ] *images of Jesus*
- [ ] *paper*
- [ ] *3 fine-tipped permanent markers*
- [ ] *1 "Gospel According to..." handout (p.50) for every 4 or 5 people*
- [ ] *pens or pencils*
- [ ] *1 "Meeting Jesus Stations" handout (p. 51)*
- [ ] *1 "Meeting Jesus Scriptures" handout (p. 52)*
- [ ] *scissors*
- [ ] *1 large tube of suntan lotion*
- [ ] *several pairs of sunglasses*
- [ ] *large bowl*
- [ ] *fish-shaped crackers*
- [ ] *placemat or tablecloth*
- [ ] *sound effects CDs that include storm or rough sea sounds*
- [ ] *CD players with headphones*
- [ ] *board game that includes play money (like the Monopoly board game)*
- [ ] *two 4x4 pieces of wood*
- [ ] *hammer*
- [ ] *small bowl*
- [ ] *1 masonry nail for each person*
- [ ] *self-adhesive notes*
- [ ] *tablecloth*
- [ ] *large candle*
- [ ] *basket*
- [ ] *1 tea light for each person*
- [ ] *matches*
- [ ] *modeling clay*

Take 44
*Blockbuster
Movie Events*

What Would Jesus Do?
Meeting Jesus in the 21st Century

The Pitch

Joshua posits what would happen if Jesus arrived in modern day Anytown, USA. This good-hearted film scratches beneath the surface of religion to the meat of authentic Christian faith, promoting loving action and unity between believers while introducing the audience to the Savior all over again.

Favorite Quote

"Simon Peter answered, 'You are the Christ, the Son of the living God'" (Matthew 16:16).

More Quotables: Matthew 4:1-3a; 11:28-30; 14:19-21; 16:13-20; 21:12-13; Mark 4:37-39; Luke 18:40-43; John 8:12; 10:17-18

Suggested Schedule

Section	Activities	Time	Supplies
The Red Carpet	*The Jesus Factor*	15-20 minutes	Bible, images of Jesus, paper, permanent-ink pens
The Production	*Joshua*	90 minutes	Movie: *Joshua*, DVD player or VCR, TV
Postproduction	*Discussion*	10-15 minutes	
	The Gospel According to...	25-30 minutes	Bible, "The Gospel According to..." handout (p. 50), pens or pencils
	Meeting Jesus Stations	35-40 minutes	"Meeting Jesus Stations" handout (p. 51), "Meeting Jesus Scriptures" handout (p. 52), scissors, suntan lotion, sunglasses, bowls, fish-shaped crackers, placemat, sound effects CDs, CD players, headphones, game board with play money, 4x4s, nails, hammer, self-adhesive notes, pens or pencils, tablecloth, candle, basket, tea lights, matches
Word of Mouth	*Molding a Friendship*	10-15 minutes	Modeling clay

Movie Review

Joshua tells the story of—duh—Joshua (Tony Goldwyn), a drifting carpenter who takes up residence in a quaint town. The new guy makes friends fast, helping Theo (Eddie Bo) rebuild the abandoned Baptist church, reaching out to troubled teen Kevin (Matt Ziegler), giving confidence to Catholic priest Father Pat (Kurt Fuller), and even catching the eye of news anchor Maggie (Stacy Edwards). The anger of the church elite comes down upon Joshua as his circle of friends grows wider and his encouragement for everyone to work together in love and unity bears fruit.

Even for those who have heard about Jesus their entire lives and have seen his life depicted countless times, it's a challenge to connect his dynamic life to our contemporary everyday existence. *Joshua* does a surprisingly good job of bridging that gap via the never predictable but always righteous person of Joshua/Jesus. Your young people will love getting to know the original revolutionary in a more familiar setting. They will leave this experience with a clearer understanding of who Jesus is and how they can incorporate his teachings into their lives.

Pastoral Guidance

Other than a few substitute curse words such as "sucks," Joshua contains nothing offensive. (See page 5 for more details.)

Preproduction

Set up a movie viewing area with the TV or projector and VCR or DVD player. Have the movie set up and ready to go.

Turn your room into an art gallery depicting Jesus. Display images, pictures, paintings, advertisements, and action figures. Make an effort to gather images that span the centuries and the globe—to have only blond-haired, blue-eyed pictures of Jesus would be missing the point. Check your local library and surf the Internet for images of Jesus, or purchase the "Christ We Share" resource with several unique pictures of Jesus from www.cms-uk.org (link to "Resources for You").

The "Meeting Jesus" stations require some careful preparation. First, you'll need to designate seven different areas within your meeting space for the stations. The stations should be easy to find but far enough apart so that several people can enjoy each station simultaneously without interfering with others.

+ Photocopy the "Meeting Jesus Stations" handout (p. 51), cut apart the instructions, and place each station's instructions prominently in one of the seven designated areas. Also photocopy the "Meeting Jesus Scriptures" handout (p. 52), cut apart the Scriptures, and place each Scripture prominently at the corresponding station.
  • For the "Temptation" station, place a tube of suntan lotion on the floor.
  • For the "Healings" station, set out a few pairs of sunglasses.

> **PRODUCTION TIP**
>
> Ask your young people to create their own interpretations of Jesus in paint, clay, film, poetry, or any other art form they enjoy. These personal expressions will make your exhibit even more powerful.

- For the "Feeding" station, place a large bowl of fish-shaped crackers on a placemat or tablecloth.
- For the "Storm" station, find a sound effects CD that includes rough sea sounds or stormy sounds—Classic Sound Effects or 150 Spectacular Sound Effects, for example. Make copies of the sound effect tracks so you can play them on "repeat." Set out several CD players with headphones.
- For the "Money-Changers" station, lay a board game like Monopoly on the floor. Set the play money on top of the board.
- For the "Cross" station, create a wooden cross from two 4x4 pieces of wood, and lean it against the wall. Secure it as necessary so it won't slide or fall. Place a bowl of masonry nails and a hammer at the base of the cross, along with self-adhesive notes and pens or pencils.
- For the "Light of the World" station, set out a tablecloth on the floor in the center of the room. Place one large candle in the center, and place a basket filled with tea lights and a large box of matches nearby.

On a table, set out enough modeling clay for each participant to have some. (You may want to keep the clay in plastic bags until you're ready to use it so that it won't dry out.)

PRODUCTION TIPS

If possible, recruit seven adult volunteers to provide direction at each "Meeting Jesus" station. These volunteers can direct young people to the station's directions and Scripture, as well as rearrange any supplies as students move in and out of the stations.

If you can't find sound effects CDs or enough CD players for your group, provide "rain sticks" at the "Storm" station instead. You can find rain sticks at nature-themed stores, or you can make your own by placing dried beans in a paper towel tube and closing off the ends with aluminum foil secured with rubber bands.

If you're not able to make the cross for the "Cross" station but can borrow a cross from the church (no matter how large or small), simply have students stick their self-adhesive notes to the cross instead of using nails.

Bonus Swag

Use these ideas to produce even more of the movie's ambience throughout this event.
- Place candles and carpentry tools around the meeting space to look like Joshua's barn.
- Have adult volunteers dress as priests—especially if at least one volunteer can wear fishing waders.

WEB SITE NOTE: *Be sure to check out www.group.com/blockbusterevents for great resources to promote and plan these events!*

The Red Carpet

As teenagers arrive, encourage them to wander around your art gallery, studying the different images of Jesus.

The Jesus Factor

Get everyone's attention, and ask teenagers to line up in three even lines. Hand each person a sheet of blank paper, and give the first person in each line a fine-tipped permanent marker.

Say: **Congratulations! You're all contestants on the "Jesus Factor," the amazing game show that tests your knowledge about Jesus! Here's how the game works. I'm going to ask a question. The person at the front of each line will write his or her answers. After five seconds, you will reveal your answers; your team will try to get the most number of correct answers. Then the next person in your line will answer the next question. If anyone shouts out or whispers an answer to a teammate, your team can't answer that question and has to wait till the next one.**

When everyone understands, ask the following questions. Allow five seconds for "contestants" to think

PRODUCTION TIP

If you have more than 15 young people, have them form additional lines. If you have fewer than nine, have them form two lines. Basically you should have between three and five people in each group.

about and write their answers between each question.

Ask: • *Was Jesus amazingly handsome?* (No—Isaiah 53:2-3.)

• *How many wise men came to visit Jesus when he was a child?* (We don't know—Matthew 2:1-2.)

• *How many men did Jesus miraculously feed with loaves and fishes?* (9,000 total—5,000 reported in Mark 6:41-44, and 4,000 reported in Mark 8:6-9.)

• *Where was Jesus raised?* (Nazareth—Matthew 2:21-23.)

• *Who were the first disciples Jesus called into ministry?* (Simon and Andrew—Mark 1:16-18.)

• *Did Jesus ever commit a sin?* (No—1 Peter 2:21-24.)

• *What Old Testament figures did Jesus speak with in front of some of his disciples?* (Moses and Elijah—Mark 9:2-4.)

Lead everyone in applause for all the contestants.

Say: **Even though countless songs, books, and movies have been created about Jesus, we still don't know a lot about him. We know some of the major things—such as exactly who Jesus is.** Ask a volunteer to read aloud Matthew 16:13-20.

Say: **We want to get to know better who Jesus is by watching** *Joshua,* **a movie that shows what might happen if Jesus were to show up today right here in our hometown. While you watch, be looking for clues about who Jesus is and what he stands for.**

The Production—*Joshua*

Gather everyone around the TV to watch the movie. Start the film, sit back, relax, and enjoy!

Postproduction

Discussion

Allow a five-minute stretch and bathroom break before gathering everyone together again. Then ask:

• *What surprised you about the movie's depiction of Jesus?*

• *What new insights did you gain about Jesus?*

• *What makes it difficult to get to know Jesus and develop a relationship with him?*

The Gospel According to...

Have young people form groups of four or five. Say: **We've just seen one person's idea about what would**

happen if Jesus visited a modern town, but what would happen if he came to our town? You're going to find out! We've heard about the Gospels according to Matthew, Mark, Luke, and John, but now's your chance to create a gospel according to you!

Ask one person in each group to be the "recorder," and distribute a "Gospel According to..." handout (p. 50) and a pen or pencil to the recorders. Have the recorders write their group members' names at the top of the page, and then ask group members for the specific types of words or phrases requested in the parentheses throughout the handout.

When everyone has finished, ask for a volunteer from each group to read aloud his or her group's "gospel." Then have groups discuss the following questions:

• *Would you want to meet Jesus if he came to our town today? Why or why not?*

• *Would you conduct yourself differently if you could see that Jesus was right here in our town, right here in this room, and right here with you? If so, how?*

• *Why don't we live every moment as if Jesus is right there with us?*

• *What are some practical ways that you can remind yourself that Jesus is with you at all times?*

• *Why do you think people believe that Jesus cares mostly about rules?*

• *Read Matthew 11:28-30 aloud. What else do you think Jesus cares about?*

Meeting Jesus Stations

Say: **We're going to get to know Jesus a little better tonight by connecting his life to our own. Several "Meeting Jesus" stations have been set up around the room. Each station relates an episode from Jesus' life to your life today. These stations give you an opportunity to think about Jesus, how his life impacts you today, and how you can connect more closely to him. The idea is that you'll make your way around the room to each station, performing the activities described for each.**

Point out the different stations to your teenagers. Then say: **You are welcome to complete the stations in any order and at any pace *except for* the "Light of the World" station.** Point out this station, and indicate that everyone is to end at that station, sitting quietly without lighting a candle until you say it's time.

Say: **I've printed the instructions for each station so you'll know what to do. There's only one rule during this time: *You must remain silent*. This is a time for personal experience and reflection. Please don't ruin someone else's experience by talking. When you've finished all but the "Light of the World" station, please sit at that station quietly.**

When everyone understands, allow students to begin circulating around the stations. Turn the lights low, with just enough light for students to read the instructions posted at each station. Plan at least 30 minutes for students to experience the stations, prompting them when only 5 minutes remain so they have time to wrap up. Tell teenagers when it's time to do the "Light of the World" activity. Afterwards, leave the lights low or operate in candlelight.

Say: **My prayer is that you've connected with Jesus tonight. Maybe you've learned something new about his character or have seen how he connects with your life today. Hopefully you're inspired to spend even more time getting to know your Savior, Jesus Christ. He's done everything he can to connect with you. All you need to do is take some time to let him in.**

Word of Mouth
Molding a Friendship

Say: **Before you leave, we're going to take a page from the movie to help you remember what you've learned about Jesus tonight. Joshua was a carpenter and sculptor. He created art to help people grow. Jesus has chosen you and calls you "friend." You're going to commemorate that friendship by sculpting something to help you remember to make Jesus a part of your life. It can be a symbol of how Jesus has reached out to you or an abstract representation of his presence in your life.**

Point out the modeling clay, and allow teenagers to create. When they've finished, allow them to take their symbols with them.

Suggested Overnight Retreat Schedule

If you'd like to extend this event into an overnight retreat, use this schedule as a starting point.

Day	Time	Activities	Supplies
Friday	7:00 p.m.-7:30 p.m.	*The Jesus Factor*	Bible, images of Jesus, paper, fine-tipped markers
	7:30 p.m.-9:00 p.m.	*Joshua*	Movie: *Joshua,* DVD player or VCR, TV
	9:00 p.m.-9:15 p.m.	*Discussion*	
	9:15 p.m.-10:00 p.m.	Snacks	
	10:00 p.m.-11:30 p.m.	Free time	
	Midnight	Lights out	
Saturday	8:00 a.m.-8:30 a.m.	Devotion	
	8:30 a.m.-9:00 a.m.	Breakfast	
	9:00 a.m.-9:45 a.m.	*The Gospel According to…* *Molding a Friendship*	Bible, "The Gospel According to…" handout (p. 50), pens or pencils Modeling clay
	9:45 a.m.-noon	Games or group activities	
	Noon-1:00 p.m.	Lunch	
	1:00 p.m.-3:00 p.m.	Free time	
	3:00 p.m.-3:40 p.m.	*Meeting Jesus Stations*	"Meeting Jesus Stations" handout (p. 51), "Meeting Jesus Scriptures" handout (p. 52), scissors, suntan lotion, sunglasses, bowls, fish-shaped crackers, placemat, sound effects CDs, CD players, headphones, game board with play money, 4x4s, nails, hammer, self-adhesive notes, pens or pencils, tablecloth, candle, basket, tea lights, matches
	3:40 p.m.-5:00 p.m.	Free time	
	5:00 p.m.-6:00 p.m.	Dinner	
	6:00 p.m.-7:30 p.m.	Worship and prayer	
	7:30 p.m.-8:00 p.m.	Pack and leave	

The Gospel According to...

When Jesus arrived in_____, the first place he went

‎ (your town)

was_____. He surprised everyone by_____.

‎ ‎ ‎ (common place for people to gather) ‎ ‎ ‎ ‎ ‎ ‎ ‎ ‎ ‎ ‎ ‎ ‎ ‎ ‎ ‎ ‎ ‎ ‎ (action)

This made_____ angry. _____

‎ ‎ ‎ ‎ ‎ ‎ ‎ ‎ ‎ ‎ ‎ ‎ (person) ‎ ‎ ‎ ‎ ‎ ‎ ‎ ‎ ‎ ‎ ‎ ‎ ‎ ‎ ‎ ‎ ‎ (he/she)

went to the police to have Jesus arrested for_____.

‎ (crime)

When the police found Jesus, he was_____. The police

‎ (action)

wouldn't arrest Jesus because_____. Jesus asked

‎ (typical excuse)

the_____, "Why do you _____

‎ ‎ ‎ ‎ ‎ ‎ ‎ ‎ (angry person) ‎ ‎ ‎ ‎ ‎ ‎ ‎ ‎ ‎ ‎ ‎ ‎ ‎ (emotion verb)

me?"_____said, "_____."

‎ ‎ ‎ ‎ ‎ ‎ ‎ (he/she) ‎ ‎ ‎ ‎ ‎ ‎ ‎ ‎ ‎ ‎ ‎ ‎ ‎ ‎ ‎ ‎ (reason)

Jesus smiled and replied, "I have come to_____."

‎ (purpose)

On Sunday, Jesus went to_____. Everyone was

‎ (location)

_____. Jesus said, "I am here to_____.

‎ ‎ ‎ ‎ (emotion) ‎ ‎ ‎ ‎ ‎ ‎ ‎ ‎ ‎ ‎ ‎ ‎ ‎ ‎ ‎ ‎ (radical or extreme action)

The people_____. The pastors in town tried to_____

‎ ‎ ‎ ‎ ‎ ‎ ‎ (verb) ‎ ‎ ‎ ‎ ‎ ‎ ‎ ‎ ‎ ‎ ‎ ‎ ‎ ‎ ‎ ‎ ‎ ‎ ‎ (verb)

Jesus. Jesus was_____but he knew he had to _____.

‎ ‎ ‎ ‎ ‎ ‎ ‎ (emotion) ‎ ‎ ‎ ‎ ‎ ‎ ‎ ‎ ‎ ‎ ‎ ‎ ‎ ‎ ‎ ‎ (verb)

Soon, people began to_____with Jesus. The town of

‎ ‎ ‎ ‎ ‎ ‎ ‎ ‎ ‎ ‎ ‎ ‎ ‎ ‎ ‎ ‎ ‎ ‎ (verb)

_____ was never the same again.

‎ ‎ (town)

Meeting Jesus Stations

- **The Temptation**—*Read the Scripture verses at this station.* Jesus was tempted in every way we are, but he didn't give in. Since he spent 40 days in the wilderness being tempted, put suntan lotion on your hands and rub it in. As the lotion covers you, pray that Jesus would protect you from the future temptations you will face.

- **The Healings**—*Read the Scripture verses at this station.* Jesus healed numerous people of several different ailments, including death! Put on a pair of sunglasses, imagining what blindness would be like—no sight for a lifetime. Remove the glasses, thank Jesus for his many miracles, and ask that he will help you see the miracles he performs around you today.

- **The Feeding**—*Read the Scripture verses at this station.* Jesus fed thousands of people with only a few fish and loaves of bread. Slowly eat some fish crackers, one by one. As you chew, thank Jesus for providing you with necessities like food. Also ask that he will help you find ways to meet the needs of less-fortunate people around you.

- **The Storm**—*Read the Scripture verses at this station.* With a simple phrase, Jesus calmed a raging storm. Put the headphones on, and listen to the pounding waves. Think about the rough times you've had. Whisper the name "Jesus," and press "pause." Pray that Jesus will bring calm to the storms in your life.

- **The Money-Changers**—*Read the Scripture verses at this station.* Jesus ran the money-changers out of the Temple because they were focused on profit instead of God. Throw a handful of play money into the air. As you pick up the bills, pray that Jesus will keep you from falling into the trap of materialism by showing you how to use the money you're blessed with wisely rather than selfishly.

- **The Cross**—*Read the Scripture verses at this station.* Jesus died on the cross so we might have eternal life with him in a relationship that continues for eternity. We can enjoy this relationship because he died on the cross and rose again. Write a thank you note to Jesus, and nail it to the cross in appreciation.

- **The Light of the World**—*Read the Scripture verse at this station.* Jesus is the light of the world. Light a match from the main candle to represent the way Jesus ignites his followers. Light a tea candle, and pray that your relationship with Jesus will shine for the world to see.

Meeting Jesus Scriptures

The Temptation—*Matthew 4:1-3a*

"Then Jesus was led by the Spirit into the desert to be tempted by the devil. After fasting forty days and forty nights, he was hungry. The tempter came to him..."

The Healings—*Luke 18:40-43*

"Jesus stopped and ordered the man to be brought to him. When he came near, Jesus asked him, 'What do you want me to do for you?'

" 'Lord, I want to see,' he replied.

"Jesus said to him, 'Receive your sight; your faith has healed you.' Immediately he received his sight and followed Jesus, praising God. When all the people saw it, they also praised God."

The Feeding—*Matthew 14:19-21*

"And he directed the people to sit down on the grass. Taking the five loaves and the two fish and looking up to heaven, he gave thanks and broke the loaves. Then he gave them to the disciples, and the disciples gave them to the people. They all ate and were satisfied, and the disciples picked up twelve basketfuls of broken pieces that were left over. The number of those who ate was about five thousand men, besides women and children."

The Storm—*Mark 4:37-39*

"A furious squall came up, and the waves broke over the boat, so that it was nearly swamped. Jesus was in the stern, sleeping on a cushion. The disciples woke him and said to him, 'Teacher, don't you care if we drown?'

"He got up, rebuked the wind and said to the waves, 'Quiet! Be still!' Then the wind died down and it was completely calm."

The Money-Changers—*Matthew 21:12-13*

"Jesus entered the temple area and drove out all who were buying and selling there. He overturned the tables of the money changers and the benches of those selling doves. 'It is written,' he said to them, ' "My house will be called a house of prayer," but you are making it a "den of robbers." ' "

The Cross—*John 10:17-18*

"The reason my Father loves me is that I lay down my life—only to take it up again. No one takes it from me, but I lay it down of my own accord. I have authority to lay it down and authority to take it up again. This command I received from my Father."

The Light of the World—*John 8:12*

"When Jesus spoke again to the people, he said, 'I am the light of the world. Whoever follows me will never walk in darkness, but will have the light of life.' "

Rating:
PG for language and some rough sports action

The Props

- ☐ *Bibles*
- ☐ *movie:* Miracle
- ☐ *DVD player or VCR*
- ☐ *TV or video projector*
- ☐ *1 "No 'I' in Team" handout (p. 59)*
- ☐ *scissors*
- ☐ *pens or pencils*
- ☐ *1 "The Part You Play" handout (p. 60) for each person*
- ☐ *newsprint*
- ☐ *tape*
- ☐ *marker*
- ☐ *1 "Gold Medal" handout (p. 61) for each person*
- ☐ *art supplies such as markers, crayons, glitter, and glue*
- ☐ *yarn*
- ☐ *hole punch*

Getting a Beautiful Body:
Working Together as a Team

The Pitch

Miracle turns one of the greatest moments in sports history into an opportunity for you to galvanize your students around working together as a team. This inspirational film portrays the goal every church has for seeing its ministry operate the way God intended, as the dynamic body of Christ.

Favorite Quote

"The body is a unit, though it is made up of many parts; and though all its parts are many, they form one body. So it is with Christ" (1 Corinthians 12:12).

More Quotables: Ecclesiastes 4:9-12; Matthew 25:14-28; Romans 12:4-8; 1 Corinthians 12:12-27

Suggested Schedule

Section	Activities	Time	Supplies
The Red Carpet	*No "I" in Team*	10-15 minutes	Bible, "No 'I' in Team" handout (p. 59), scissors
The Production	*Miracle*	135 minutes	Movie: *Miracle*, DVD player or VCR, TV
Postproduction	*Discussion*	10-15 minutes	
	The Part You Play	25-30 minutes	Bible, "The Part You Play" handout (p. 60), pens or pencils, newsprint, tape, marker
Word of Mouth	*Reaching for Gold*	5-10 minutes	"Gold Medal" handout (p. 61), art supplies, scissors, yarn, hole punch

Take 54
Blockbuster Movie Events

Movie Review

Miracle re-enacts one of the greatest moments in U.S. sports history. Herb Brooks (Kurt Russell) asks for the impossible task of turning a disparate group of college students—players he handpicked who weren't necessarily the country's best—into a hockey team that must compete against the greatest in the world at the 1980 Olympics. Brooks puts his team through intense training, molding them into a family that sleeps, eats, plays, and suffers together. Through his tough love, he transforms the ragtag group of players who hate each other into a tightknit, well-oiled machine ready to take on the world.

Hopefully your students aren't throwing off the gloves; if so, you're starting a step ahead of Herb Brooks in forming your winning team. *Miracle* inspires even the most cynical heart to consider what can happen when people join together under a common purpose. After enjoying this event, your young people will experience a tighter bond with one another, have a clearer vision of the benefits of teamwork when working for the kingdom of God, and clarify their own roles in creating such a team.

Pastoral Guidance

Miracle contains a couple dozen "hells" and several scenes that include social drinking of beer, though there's no drunkenness depicted. (See page 5 for more details or visit www.screenit.com for a detailed list of the film's content.)

Preproduction

Set up a movie viewing area with the TV or projector and VCR or DVD player. Have the movie set up and ready to go.

Photocopy the "No 'I' in Team" handout (p. 59), and cut it into 12 squares.

Tape a sheet of newsprint to a wall; on it, list each ministry that your group currently is involved in. Leave room under each ministry to write names, and leave room at the bottom to add new ministries. Cover up this list until you're ready to use it.

Set up a table with art supplies—markers, crayons, glitter, glue, yarn, scissors, and hole punch—for students to decorate "gold medals."

Bonus Swag

Use these ideas to produce even more of the movie's ambience throughout this event.
- *If you want to get incredibly authentic, crank down the air conditioner so it's noticeably chilly, and provide hot chocolate to warm up.*
- *Purchase or create tiny American flags, and hand them out for each person to wave during the climactic scene in the movie.*
- *Create banners depicting the Olympic rings and "U.S.A." Find some American and Soviet flags to hang from the ceiling.*

WEB SITE NOTE: *Be sure to check out www.group.com/blockbusterevents for great resources to promote and plan these events!*

The Red Carpet

No "I" in Team

Have students form groups of five or six, and give each group one of the cards from the "No 'I' In Team" handout (p. 59). Have groups discuss these questions:

- *Do you like working as part of a team, or do you prefer to work independently? Why?*
- *What's the most difficult thing about working in a team?*
- *Read Ecclesiastes 4:9-12. What are some advantages to working in a team?*

Say: **Your card lists a machine or situation that's missing something. In the next five minutes, your group needs to create a short skit that shows everyone what that machine or situation would be like without the missing item.**

As teams work, circulate to answer questions and check their progress. After five minutes, call everyone back together. Then have each team take a turn performing its skit, first explaining the setting so that the audience can guess what's missing after the skit. After each team's performance, lead the audience in applauding before inviting students to guess what was missing. Then ask a volunteer to read aloud 1 Corinthians 12:12-27, and have teams discuss these questions:

- *What were the effects when even small components of a machine or situation were missing?*
- *How is this similar to what happens when the body of Christ is missing someone's participation?*
- *What are some reasons people give for not using their gifts as part of the Church?*

After the discussion, say: **We're going to see the true story of an amazing group of men who accomplished the impossible through dedicated teamwork. As we watch *Miracle*, be thinking about the church and how we are supposed to be functioning like an Olympic-caliber team.**

The Production—*Miracle*

Gather everyone around the TV to watch the movie. Start the film, sit back, relax, and enjoy!

Postproduction

Discussion

After the movie ends, allow a five-minute stretch and bathroom break. When everyone has returned, ask:

- *What issues kept the hockey players from becoming a team immediately?*
- *What helped them to overcome those hurdles?*
- *How could Christians in a church function like a team?*
- *What issues keep us from becoming a team here in the church?*
- *What could help bring us together?*

The Part You Play

Say: **It's important that every church function as a team. God assembled each of us here just as Herb Brooks carefully selected the members of his team for a purpose. God knows our character and talent as our creator, so we have everything we need to be part of a miracle!**

Ask a volunteer to read aloud Matthew 25:14-28. Then have groups discuss these questions:

- *Why does God get so angry with us for not using our talents?*
- *What message are you sending to God when you bury your talents?*
- *What do you think could happen if we all worked as a team, using our talents for God's glory?*

- *What hurdles might prevent us from working together as a team?*
- *How can we knock down those barriers?*

Distribute the "Part You Play" handouts (p. 60) and pens or pencils.

Say: **We're going to find out what "position" you're best suited for on our team. Work independently to fill out the information on this sheet. In a few minutes, we'll discuss what you discover. Go ahead and find out the part you play!**

After about five minutes, bring everyone back together. Reveal the sheet of newsprint you created before the event with the list of ministries written on it.

Say: **This is a list of ministries teenagers in the church are involved in. You might immediately see a place where you can use your talent, and that's great. You might not see anything that matches what you've identified as the part you play. That could mean you're here to start that ministry!**

Explain that you're going to call out each ministry and that students should call out their names if their gifts fit that ministry. Assure your students that multiple names can appear under each ministry and that their names can appear multiple times on the list. After you've gone through the list, ask for ideas about new or different ministries that students have thought about. Be sure each young person is listed at least once.

Afterward, ask a volunteer to read aloud Romans 12:4-8. Say: **God commands us to use our gifts. As you can see, God has assembled a gold medal team right here!**

Have students form groups according to the ministries they thought their talents could assist. Students whose names appear under more than one list should gather with the smaller group. If students are the only ones listed, ask them to meet with you. Encourage groups to discuss how they can work together as a team, using their talents to take the ministry to the next level.

After five minutes, ask everyone to come back together and share how his or her position is going to make the team better. Allow each position to share, and be sure to support each idea.

Word of Mouth
Reaching for Gold

Distribute a "Gold Medal" handout (p. 61) to each person, and set out the art supplies. Ask everyone to pair up with a friend. Then say: **Each and every one of you is worthy of a gold medal on God's team. God has placed immense talent in you—talent that you can't hide. Now is the time to put those talents to use, pushing our team to do the impossible with God's help.**

Explain that teenagers will fill in the medal with the names of their partners and then the categories for which they're receiving their medals. Say: **Each of you brings something special to the body of Christ. Maybe it's encouragement or humor or a servant heart or singing. Whatever spiritual quality you see in your partner, write it on the medal. Use the art supplies provided to decorate the medal any way you want. After you've finished, cut it out and use yarn so you'll be able to tie it around your partner's neck. You'll have five minutes to decorate your medal, and then we'll have an awards ceremony.**

Warn everyone when the time's almost up. After five minutes, bring everyone back together in one large group. Have pairs take turns standing up, putting the medals around their partners' necks, and saying what their partners received medals for.

SPECIAL EFFECTS

As people receive their medals, play John Williams' "Summon the Heroes" from the *American Journey* CD.

Say: **Look around you. We have a great team in place! Working together, we can accomplish anything God places before us. And now the entire body of Christ knows about your gifts and talents, and we can encourage each other to use those talents.**

Have teenagers join hands, and close by praying for direction and wisdom on how the group can work together for God's glory.

Suggested Overnight Retreat Schedule

If you'd like to extend this event into an overnight retreat, use this schedule as a starting point.

Day	Time	Activities	Supplies
Friday	7:00 p.m.-7:30 p.m.	Team games	
	7:30 p.m.-9:45 p.m.	*Miracle*	Movie: *Miracle*, DVD player or VCR, TV
	9:45 p.m.-10:00 p.m.	*Discussion*	
	10:00 p.m.-11:30 p.m.	Free time	Pens or pencils, paper
	Midnight	Lights out	
Saturday	8:00 a.m.-8:30 a.m.	Devotion	
	8:30 a.m.-9:00 a.m.	Breakfast	
	9:00 a.m.-9:15 a.m.	*No "I" in Team*	Bible, "No 'I' in Team" handout (p. 59), scissors
	9:15 a.m.-noon	Games or group activities	
	Noon-1:00 p.m.	Lunch	
	1:00 p.m.-3:00 p.m.	Free time	
	3:00 p.m.-3:40 p.m.	*The Part You Play* *Reaching for Gold*	Bible, "The Part You Play" handout (p. 60), pens or pencils, newsprint, tape, marker "Gold Medal" handout (p. 61), art supplies, scissors, yarn, hole punch
	3:40 p.m.-5:00 p.m.	Free time	
	5:00 p.m.-6:00 p.m.	Dinner	
	6:00 p.m.-7:30 p.m.	Worship and prayer	
	7:30 p.m.-8:00 p.m.	Pack and leave	

No "I" in Team

A car that's missing a steering wheel.

A football team that's missing a quarterback.

A fast-food drive-through that's missing a microphone.

A sailing team that's missing wind.

A choir comprised only of sopranos.

A team of firefighters without water.

A race car pit crew with no tires.

A cell phone that's missing the antenna.

A skateboard with no ball bearings.

A softball diamond that's missing first base.

The Part You Play

1 Corinthians 12:12

1. Check all that you're interested in:

☐ missions	☐ healing
☐ prayer	☐ hospitality
☐ creativity	☐ faith
☐ discernment	☐ mercy
☐ giving	☐ administration
☐ leadership	☐ serving
☐ wisdom	☐ knowledge
☐ encouragement	☐ teaching
☐ music	☐ pastoring
☐ evangelism	☐ prophecy

2. What talents do you have? _____

3. What hobbies do you have? _____

4. What is the most important part of your Christian walk?

☐ singing praise	☐ Bible study
☐ prayer	☐ helping the poor
☐ evangelism	☐ hospitality

5. In your opinion, which area of our ministry needs the most help, or what area

are we completely ignoring? _____

Gold Medal

1 Corinthians 12:12

Presented to:

In recognition of:

Gold Medal

Rating:
PG

The Props

- ☐ *Bibles*
- ☐ *movie: The Mission*
- ☐ *DVD player or VCR*
- ☐ *TV or video projector*
- ☐ *lyrics to the hymn "Amazing Grace"*
- ☐ *candy or gum as a prize*
- ☐ *1 card from the "Tyrant Cards" handout (p. 68) for each person*
- ☐ *scissors*
- ☐ *2 clip-on ties, briefcase, and fancy blouse*
- ☐ *desk and chair*
- ☐ *1 self-adhesive note for each person*
- ☐ *pens or pencils*
- ☐ *cinder blocks (available at Home Depot or other hardware stores)*
- ☐ *large cross at least 6 feet high—free-standing, painted on a wall, or made from butcher paper*
- ☐ *1 white athletic wristband for each person*
- ☐ *colorful permanent markers*

Forgiving the Thief:
God's Amazing Grace

The Pitch

The Mission paints a stirring picture of grace. All human beings, no matter how repulsive, can receive grace by humbling themselves before God. Your young people will learn about grace—how to receive it themselves and how to extend it to others.

Favorite Quote

"For it is by grace you have been saved, through faith—and this not from yourselves, it is the gift of God—not by works, so that no one can boast. For we are God's workmanship, created in Christ Jesus to do good works, which God prepared in advance for us to do" (Ephesians 2:8-10).

More Quotables: Isaiah 1:16-18; Matthew 11:28-30; 18:23-35; Luke 23:39-43; Acts 9:1-19; Ephesians 2:1-10

Suggested Schedule

Section	Activities	Time	Supplies
The Red Carpet	*Amazing Grace*	10-15 minutes	Lyrics to the song "Amazing Grace," candy or gum
The Production	*The Mission*	120 minutes	Movie: *The Mission*, DVD player or VCR, TV
Postproduction	*Discussion*	10-15 minutes	Bibles
	Has Anyone Seen Grace?	30-35 minutes	Bibles, "Tyrant Cards" handout (p. 68), scissors, clip-on ties, blouse, briefcase, desk, chair
	Dropping Weight	10-15 minutes	Bible, self-adhesive notes, pens or pencils, cinder blocks, large cross
Word of Mouth	*Gracelets*	5-10 minutes	Bible, wristbands, permanent markers

Movie Review

The Mission is a stunning achievement both as a film and as a statement of faith. The film follows Father Gabriel (Jeremy Irons), a Jesuit priest who sets up a mission among a remote tribe in the jungles of South America. Rodrigo Mendoza (Robert De Niro), a notorious slave trader, joins the Jesuit order after murdering his own brother. His transformation from a cold blooded mercenary to a man of God exemplifies the power of grace and the gospel. This paradise on earth, where "savages" and "saints" live together in peace, falls into jeopardy when the Catholic Church agrees to hand sovereignty of the missions from Spain to slavery-condoning Portugal. A war over the physical bodies of the spiritually redeemed people results.

Grace separates Christianity from all other religions. Jesus extends forgiveness and adoption into his family to all who repent of their sin and ask his help. After experiencing *The Mission*, your students will understand the radical nature of God's grace, how they can receive it in their lives, and how they can extend it to others.

Pastoral Guidance

The Mission is exceptionally clean except for some "native" nudity. A real tribe, the Waunana, portrays the Guarani tribe that the film is about. The Waunana may or may not wear clothing, as they choose; children run around without clothing, and women don't wear tops. None of this is shown sensuously or gratuitously. Also, Rodrigo catches his brother in bed with his ex-girlfriend (25:40). Though details aren't apparent, it is obvious that the couple is nude. (See page 5 for more details or visit www.screenit.com for a detailed list of the film's content.)

Preproduction

Set up a movie viewing area with the TV or projector and VCR or DVD player. Have the movie set up and ready to go.

Photocopy the "Tyrant Cards" handout, and cut them out so that each person will have one card.

Position a desk and chair in the area of your meeting space where you'll direct the "Ungrateful Employee" skit. The desk and chair should be angled toward the audience.

Stack the cinder blocks in a corner. If you have more participants than you have cinder blocks, simply reuse them. On the opposite side of the room from the cinder blocks, set up a large cross—a free-standing cross, one that's painted on the wall, or even one made from butcher paper. The cross should be at least 6 feet high.

Bonus Swag

Use these ideas to produce even more of the movie's ambience throughout this event.
- *Turn your meeting area into a jungle. Cover your walls in butcher paper, and have students paint jungle murals on the paper. Or cover the walls in black plastic or butcher paper, and set many plants, ficus trees, and other foliage on the floor in front of the walls.*

- *Roll up brown butcher paper and tape it to a wall to serve as a tree trunk. Cut out "leaves" from green butcher paper, and attach them to the trunk.*
- *Have adult volunteers dress as Jesuit priests with brown robes, black skull caps, and bare feet.*
- *Play a sound effects CD with jungle noises such as frogs, insects, rain, and waterfalls.*

WEB SITE NOTE: *Be sure to check out www.group.com/blockbusterevents for great resources to promote and plan these events!*

The Red Carpet
Amazing Grace

After everyone has arrived, say: **Welcome to the South American jungle! We're going to see how God's grace can penetrate the deepest, darkest jungle. Before we enter the jungle, we're going to have a quick contest!**

I want everyone to stand up with me. We're all going to sing the hymn "Amazing Grace" together. We'll start with the familiar first verse and then sing the other verses. If you sing the wrong words or get to a part of the song you don't know, sit down. We'll sing the hymn all the way through and see who's left standing.

Lead the group in singing "Amazing Grace." If more than one person is left standing, have them split the prize.

Then say: **We can't talk about God's amazing grace and leave anyone empty-handed. With grace, everyone's a winner!** Toss the prize into the group, making sure everyone receives something.

Say: **That's the great thing about grace. Not everyone may deserve it—just as you didn't deserve the prize based on my initial guidelines. However, everyone who asks for grace can have it. The writer of "Amazing Grace" knew that better than anyone else. John Newton was the captain of a ship that transported slaves from Africa to America. He was also known to use exceptionally filthy language and indulge in several vices. (Remember, he was a**

sailor.) **Though he grew up a Christian and often made promises to serve God in times of trouble or desperation, he always slipped back into old patterns.**

Captain Newton finally committed himself completely to God, eventually quitting his job transporting slaves. A few years later, looking back on his life of sin and debauchery, he penned the lyrics Christians around the world have been singing for more than 200 years.

The reality of grace, both the perfect kind that God extends to humanity and the imperfect grace people extend to one another, is truly an amazing sight to behold. You're going to receive a graduate-level course on grace as we journey back in time and to the jungles of South America with *The Mission.*

The Production—
The Mission

Gather everyone around the TV to watch the movie. Start the film, sit back, relax, and enjoy!

SPECIAL EFFECTS

If possible, view the film in widescreen because the jungle and waterfall shots are breathtaking.

Postproduction
Discussion

Allow a five-minute stretch and bathroom break. When everyone has returned, have students form groups of six to discuss these questions:

- *Did Rodrigo deserve the grace he received? Why or why not?*
- *What other characters did despicable things in the film? Do you think they could ever receive grace for their horrible deeds? Why or why not?*
- *Read Ephesians 2:1-10. What hits you most about this passage?*
- *After reading Ephesians 2:1-10, how would you define grace?*
- *What makes the action of extending grace counter to our natural instincts?*
- *How would the world change if people decided to show grace toward one another? What prevents people from showing grace?*

Has Anyone Seen Grace?

Have teenagers stay in their groups, and give each group a set of "Tyrant Cards" (p. 68) so that every person has one card. Have students share the contents of their cards with each other before discussing the following questions:

- *What's your reaction to these "tyrants"?*
- *What's your reaction to the idea of extending grace to these folks if they were to repent and ask forgiveness?*
- *Read Luke 23:39-43. Why did Jesus show grace to the thief?*
- *Does everyone receive God's grace? Why or why not? What must a person do to receive grace?*
- *How can grace change someone's life?*
- *What prayer would you offer regarding the tyrant on your card?*

Say: **We may not have a problem extending grace to our friends and family members when they ask for forgiveness, but it's often a different story when someone who has truly caused widespread suffering repents. It may not seem fair that God grants perfect grace at any time in a person's life, no matter what he or she has done. But God's grace is so strong that it seems to shine most brightly when people with a mountain of offenses—like the thief on the cross—receive it. History is littered with people who have been profoundly affected by this holy display of forgiveness. One of the most dramatic turnarounds happened to a man named Saul.** Ask a volunteer to read aloud Acts 9:1-19. Then have groups discuss these questions:

- *Why do you think God chose such an evil man to be his representative to the Gentiles?*
- *What does Saul's story say about the nature of grace and how it works in a person's life?*
- *How have you personally experienced grace?*
- *Has grace changed you? If so, how?*

Say: **When people experience grace, they shouldn't keep it all to themselves. Jesus taught people to pass along grace through a great story in Matthew 18:23-35.**

Ask for two guys and one girl to volunteer to help tell the story. Give the guys clip-on ties to wear, hand one a briefcase to carry, and have the girl put on the fancy blouse. Explain that the three volunteers haven't heard the story you're going to read and don't know how it's going to turn out. Have the person with the briefcase play the part of Jack, and have the other guy sit at the desk.

Say: **In this drama, I'll read a line, and they're going to repeat after me—almost like the Simon Says school of acting. Everyone else needs to pay attention, too, because the audience will need to respond to cues to react. I am pleased to present you Jesus' amazing story about the ungrateful employee!**

When everyone understands, read the following script with pauses to allow the actors to repeat after you.

Bill Gates is really, really rich. He sits behind a huge desk making big decisions. Bigger decisions. One day, he decided to settle his accounts. He said, "Hey, Jack! Come in here!" Jack came in, skipping. I'm just kidding. He's a professional! Jack went outside the office and walked back in. Bill said, "Have a seat." Jack said, "Thank you, sir," and sat down.

Bill stood up. "Jack, you borrowed a million dollars last year. It's time to pay up." Jack was startled. Then he was angry. Finally, he started crying like a baby. He stopped crying and said, "There is no way. . .I can pay back. . .all that money at once." Bill sighed. Louder. He crossed his arms. The other way. He said, "I guess you and your family. . .will be my slaves."

Jack got on his knees. He grabbed Bill around the legs. Not so tight. He begged, "Please, Mr. Gates! Have patience! I promise to repay everything." Bill put one hand over his heart and patted Jack's head with the other. "I pity you. I want to forgive your debt. You don't owe a thing."

Jack leapt up in joy. He leapt higher. Everyone in the office cheered! Jack gave Bill a hug. He gave Bill a kiss! JUST KIDDING! He said, "Thanks, Boss. I'll never forget this." Jack left the office.

Outside the office, Jack saw Katy. "Hey, Katy!" he shouted. Louder. "Hi," Katy replied. Jack put his arm around Katy. The other arm. He said, "Do you have that five bucks you owe me?" She shook her head. "I won't have it until payday." Jack GENTLY choked her. He screamed, "Pay back what you owe!"

Katy fell to her knees. She grabbed Jack's legs. "Please, Jack," she begged. "Have patience! I promise to repay everything." Jack put one hand over his heart and patted Kat y's head with the other.

"I pity you Katy, because I'm taking you to court . . . and suing for everything you've got!"

Everyone in the office booed. They hissed. They told Bill Gates what happened. They stopped telling him. Bill Gates came out and grabbed Jack. He said, "You wicked man. I forgave your million-dollar debt. Why didn't you forgive Katy's five dollars? I showed you great mercy, and you should have done the same."

Some people from the office grabbed Jack. They dragged him off to jail. Jail is the other way. They dragged him to jail because he could not pay back the million dollars he owed. Bill shook his head sadly. More sadly. He said, "What an ungrateful employee."

Say: **Let's give our actors a hand as they return to their seats!**

Applaud the actors, then have students get back into their groups to discuss these questions:

- *Have you ever been like Jack and withheld grace from someone? If so, why?*
- *What does extending grace teach others about God?*
- *What does extending grace do for your relationship with God?*
- *How can you remember the grace God has shown you?*

Dropping Weight

Say: **The message of God's grace is so radical that it's almost impossible to believe when you hear it.**

Ask a volunteer to read aloud Matthew 11:28-30. Then distribute a self-adhesive note and a pen or pencil to each person.

Say: **Right now, we're all going to drag what's weighing us down to the cross on the other side of the room just as Rodrigo dragged his armor through the jungle. Each of you can find relief from what weighs you down when you lay it at the cross.** Have teenagers write what's weighing them down on their notes—addictions, repetitive sins, disbelief, pride,

a person, and so on. Then have them fold their notes and stick them to a cinder block.

When everyone has finished, say: **Now carry your block to the foot of the cross, and set it down. Stick the weight you wrote down on the cross. Close your eyes as you feel your arms relax from releasing the weight. Then offer a prayer to God about the grace extended to you.**

Word of Mouth
Gracelets

When everyone has finished praying and is still gathered at the cross, say: **Grace is so transcendent, so unbelievable, that people often think it doesn't apply to them after they make a blunder. Some day, you'll make a mistake, and you might believe it's so bad that you could never be forgiven. That's not true! As Rodrigo Mendoza or King David or Paul learned, God's grace is always available.**

Ask someone to read aloud Isaiah 1:16-18 for the group. Say: **God promises to wash "as white as snow" the sins of those who turn to him. To remember this verse and to remember that God's grace is always available, we're going to make "gracelets."**

Distribute the wristbands, and tell teenagers to draw a picture or symbol of God's grace on them. Say: **It might be a cross or "E289" for the Ephesians verse or even Rodrigo's sword. Make the symbol memorable so you never forget the power of God's grace.**

When students finish their gracelets, allow them to leave.

Suggested Overnight Retreat Schedule

If you'd like to extend this event into an overnight retreat, use this schedule as a starting point.

Day	Time	Activities	Supplies
Friday	7:00 p.m.-7:30 p.m.	Paint a jungle mural.	
	7:30 p.m.-9:30 p.m.	*The Mission*	Movie: *The Mission*, DVD player or VCR, TV
	9:30 p.m.-9:45 p.m.	*Discussion*	Bibles
	9:45 p.m.-10:15 p.m.	Snacks	
	10:15 p.m.-11:30 p.m.	Free time	
	Midnight	Lights out	
Saturday	8:00 a.m.-8:30 a.m.	Devotion	
	8:30 a.m.-9:00 a.m.	Breakfast	
	9:00 a.m.-10:00 a.m.	*Amazing Grace*	Lyrics to the song "Amazing Grace," candy or gum
		Has Anyone Seen Grace?	"Tyrant Cards" handout (p. 68), scissors, newsprint, marker, two clip-on ties, blouse, high-heeled shoes, desk, chair
	10:00 a.m.-noon	Games or group activities	
	Noon-1:00 p.m.	Lunch	
	1:00 p.m.-3:00 p.m.	Free time	
	3:00 p.m.-3:25 p.m.	*Dropping Weight*	Bible, self-adhesive notes, pens or pencils, cinder blocks, large cross
		Gracelets	Bible, wristbands, permanent markers
	3:25 p.m.-5:00 p.m.	Free time	
	5:00 p.m.-6:00 p.m.	Dinner	
	6:00 p.m.-7:30 p.m.	Worship and prayer	
	7:30 p.m.-8:00 p.m.	Pack and leave	

Tyrant Cards

Joseph Stalin
Posts: Soviet premier and general secretary
of the Communist Party of the Union of Soviet
Socialist Republics
Length of Rule: 1922-1953
Type of Rule: Communist dictatorship

Adolf Hitler
Post: Chancellor of Germany
Length of Rule: 1933-1945
Type of Rule: Nazi dictatorship

Saddam Hussein
Post: President of Iraq
Length of Rule: 1979-2003
Type of Rule: Military dictatorship

Osama bin Ladin
Post: Founder and leader of al-Qaeda, a
fundamentalist Islamic terrorist organization
Beginning of al-Queda leadership: 1988
Type of Leadership: Terrorism

Mao Tse-tung (Mao Zedong)
Post: Chairman of the People's
Republic of China
Length of Rule: 1949-1976
Type of Rule: Maoist Communism

Kim Jong-il
Post: Leader of North Korea
Length of Rule: 1994-present
Type of Rule: Centralized Communism

The Props

- ☐ *Bibles*
- ☐ *movie: Seabiscuit*
- ☐ *DVD player or VCR*
- ☐ *TV or video projector*
- ☐ *paper*
- ☐ *markers*
- ☐ *tape*
- ☐ *several "horses"— tricycles, skateboards, or scooters*
- ☐ *1 "Human Resources" handout (p. 75) for every 3 or 4 people*
- ☐ *pens or pencils*
- ☐ *1 bandage for each person*
- ☐ *fine-tipped markers*
- ☐ *enough photocopies of the "Get Out of Jail Free" handout (p. 76) for each person to have a few cards*
- ☐ *scissors*

Damaged Goods Welcome:
The God of Second Chances

The Pitch

Seabiscuit takes an inspiring page from history to illustrate that every person has worth, no matter how broken, bruised, or beaten up. God not only loves and accepts all these people, but also repairs them and sends them out to do great and mighty things.

Favorite Quote

"For there is no difference between Jew and Gentile—the same Lord is Lord of all and richly blesses all who call on him, for, 'Everyone who calls on the name of the Lord will be saved'" (Romans 10:12-13).

More Quotables: Luke 15:11-32; John 21:15-19; Romans 10:8-13; Galatians 6:1-4

Suggested Schedule

Section	Activities	Time	Supplies
The Red Carpet	*Horse Races*	5-10 minutes	Paper, markers, tape, children's toys as "horses"
The Production	*Seabiscuit*	150 minutes	Movie: *Seabiscuit*, DVD player or VCR, TV
Postproduction	*Discussion*	10-15 minutes	
	Human Resources	20-25 minutes	Bibles, marker, "Human Resources" handout (p. 75), pens or pencils
	Eternal Bandages	5 minutes	Bible, bandages, markers
Word of Mouth	*Get Out of Jail Free*	5 minutes	Bible, "Get Out of Jail Free" handout (p. 76), scissors

Movie Review

Seabiscuit re-creates the national frenzy surrounding the incredible accomplishments of a long-shot racehorse. From the rubble of the Great Depression, a trio of damaged men (with their horse) emerge to offer hope to the hopeless masses. Millionaire Charles Howard (Jeff Bridges), devastated by the death of his son; horse trainer Tom Smith (Chris Cooper), a cowboy cast off by the modern world; and jockey Red Pollard (Tobey Maguire), far too tall and blind in one eye, intersect to transform a small, has-been horse named Seabiscuit into a national racing sensation.

This inspirational film promotes a message (and I'm not talking about gambling on horse racing) everyone in the church should live by: You don't throw away a whole life because it's banged up a bit. The four main characters in the film, including the horse, prove that "damaged goods" can achieve great things. Jesus turns the "bottom of the barrel" into the "cream of the crop," so the church should welcome those scraping bottom. Through this event, your students will understand that all people—no matter what hurts they've inflicted upon themselves or suffered at the hands of others—can find a second chance in God's family. God heals his followers so they can impact the world.

Pastoral Guidance

Seabiscuit contains several profanities, including about a dozen variations of the s-word, a handful of "SOBs," and almost a dozen uses of the Lord's name. Also be aware of one scene that takes place in a bordello (32:45–34:30). Women wear only lingerie (though they're more covered than Britney). Red talks with the prostitute he has hired, and she undresses to reveal her bare back. (See page 5 for more details or visit www.screenit.com for a detailed list of the film's content.)

Preproduction

Set up a movie viewing area with the TV or projector and VCR or DVD player. Have the movie set up and ready to go.

Make a "racetrack" outside on grass or a parking lot. Mark a circular track with chalk, tape, or folding chairs. Gather whatever children's toys you can find to be "horses"—tricycles (funniest), skateboards (which jockeys will sit on and push with their hands), or scooters (easiest to find but more likely to promote testosterone-fueled competition). Line up the "horses" at the starting line, and recruit adult volunteers to help keep the races from getting out of hand. Have paper and markers nearby for students to create their racing numbers and logos.

Make a copy of the "Human Resources" handout (p. 75) for each group. Make enough copies of the "Get Out of Jail Free" handout (p. 76) for each person to receive at least two business cards. (If possible, copy the handout onto card stock.) Cut apart the cards.

Bonus Swag

Use these ideas to produce even more of the movie's ambience throughout this event.
- *Use an instant or digital camera to capture "photo finishes" of the horse races.*
- *Have your adult volunteers dress as jockeys or Depression-era farmers (with overalls and caps).*

- *Place around the meeting area horseshoes, buckets, saddles, and any other horse-related items you can find.*
- *Set up a table near the "racetrack" as a "bread line." Set out paper plates, biscuits or another bread item, and cups of hot tea or coffee. (If you want to go upscale, add some soup!) Begin the event by having entrants go first to the bread line while they wait for the horse races to begin. Be sure to explain that bread lines were commonplace features of the Great Depression, set up to feed families affected by the high unemployment rate.*

WEB SITE NOTE: *Be sure to check out www.group.com/blockbusterevents for great resources to promote and plan these events!*

The Red Carpet
Horse Races

Don't allow anyone to enter the room where you'll be viewing the movie. Instead, send participants to the "racetrack." Give each entrant two pieces of paper and a marker with which to create a race number and their very own racing logo. When everyone has arrived, say: **Welcome to the Great Depression of the 1930s. During this difficult era, horse racing was a popular form of entertainment. We're going to experience its thrill!**

When everyone is ready, point out the racetrack. Say: **You jockeys are going to compete in our very own Kentucky Derby! First, help each other tape the numbers on your backs and your logos to your fronts.**

As students tape on their numbers and logos, say: **As you can see, we have your "horses" ready for you at the starting line. Everyone will take a turn racing a horse around the course. We're going to take the top three finishers of each race on to the next round, and we'll keep racing until there's only one person left. Everyone will get a chance to race. Let's have our first batch of jockeys**

up to the starting line!

After the race, say: **Now that we've all experienced the life of a Depression-era horse jockey, we'll be able to relate better to the people in the film Seabiscuit. As you watch, be on the lookout for people who get second chances.**

The Production—*Seabiscuit*

Gather everyone around the TV to watch the movie. Start the film, sit back, relax, and enjoy!

Postproduction
Discussion

When the movie ends, allow a five-minute break. After five minutes, gather everyone back together.
Ask:
- *How do you think people generally respond to those they consider to be "broken"?*
- *Why do you think people have that reaction?*
- *What's your reaction to the second, third, fourth chances that people in this movie received?*
- *Do you think the church does a good job of welcoming broken people and giving them a second chance? Why or why not?*

Human Resources

Have teenagers form groups of three or four. Distribute a pen or pencil and a copy of the "Human Resources" handout (p. 75) to each group. Say: **You're the committee in charge of hiring a new pastor, and these are the people who have applied. As a group, read the descriptions and agree upon which people** you would call in for face-to-face interviews. After you've done that, look up the Scripture passages and write in each person's name. You have only five minutes to hire a quality pastor!

After five minutes, ask volunteers to share with the large group whether they were surprised by any of the résumés. Then have students each share just with their group members one thing they'd be embarrassed to include in their résumés. After people have had time to share, say: **Everyone makes mistakes, and even many of our greatest Bible heroes committed horrible acts—murder, adultery, deceit. That's what makes God so amazing. God not only grants second chances, but he also uses what may seem like the worst people for the greatest impact. Every person in the world has the opportunity to be a "Seabiscuit," rescued from brokenness and given a special role in God's family.**

One of the most famous "Seabiscuits" in Scripture is the prodigal son. Have groups refer to Luke 15:11-32 but write the story in their own words on the backs of their handouts. After about five minutes, ask groups to discuss these questions:

- *How was the son a "Seabiscuit"?*
- *Why do you think the father was willing to give his son a second chance after his horrible behavior?*
- *Does the church typically react like the father or the older brother when it comes to prodigals?* Explain.
- *Why do you think that's the reaction?*
- *Do you think a person can do anything so awful that Jesus won't offer a second chance? Why or why not?*
- *What keeps some people in the pigsty, refusing to turn to Jesus for a second chance?*
- *How can someone receive a second chance?*

Say: **Christianity is all about second chances. Maybe you've never looked at it that way, but the fact is that Jesus founded the church on this principle. Let me explain: Just hours before Jesus was crucified, his disciple Peter denied even knowing him. Read John 21:15-19 in your groups to see Jesus' later reaction to Peter.** After groups have had a chance to read, ask them to discuss these questions.

- *What's your reaction to Jesus' decision to build his church through the man who'd denied knowing him in his greatest hour of need?*
- *What kinds of mistakes or hardships do Christians find difficult to forget?*
- *What effects does dwelling upon these mistakes have?*
- *What do you think Jesus would say to someone haunted by a mistake?*

Eternal Bandages

Say: **One of the reasons people don't feel the freedom to accept a second chance is that Christians often pretend to be perfect. We pretend we don't make mistakes and that no one has ever battered or broken our spirits. This lie of perfection can make some people feel ashamed of past mistakes or hurtful experiences and can fool them into believing they aren't good enough to do the great things God has planned for them.**

Ask a volunteer to read aloud Galatians 6:1-4. Then have groups discuss these questions:

- *Why do you think people are reluctant to share their "wounds" with others—whether the wounds are mistakes they've made or hurts they've suffered?*
- *How could their sharing positively affect them? How could their sharing positively affect the church?*
- *What burden do you need help carrying?*
- *What are some practical ways we can help support each other?*

As groups discuss, distribute bandages and fine-tipped markers. After a few minutes of discussion, instruct young people to use the markers to write something on the bandages to remind them of the second chance Jesus offers—a Scripture reference, a word, or a symbol, for example.

Say: **Jesus heals our wounds. Put on your bandages so we can see that everyone in here is a "Seabiscuit"— a little banged up but ready for a second chance to win the race.**

> ### SPECIAL EFFECTS
>
> Play the clip of Peter betraying Jesus in *The Passion of the Christ* (R) that runs from 29:00–30:45 as a prelude to the discussion about Peter's second chance.

Word of Mouth

Get Out of Jail Free

Say: People are dying for a second chance because they suffer under the weight of past mistakes. Just think: They might think something they did 20 years ago has disqualified them from redemption! You have the opportunity to share the wonderful message that God loves them and gladly offers a second chance. Just imagine how many spiritual "Seabiscuits" we'd have running around here if people truly took this radical message to heart!

Ask someone to read aloud Romans 10:8-13.

Say: Jesus is waiting patiently, as did the father of the prodigal son. He's hoping all of his sons and daughters will return to him for a second chance, no matter what they've done. To help you remember this message for yourself and to share it with others, we have some "Get Out of Jail Free" cards for you to keep in your purse or wallet.

Hand out the cards to everyone. Once you've distributed them, close in a prayer of thanksgiving for the second chance Jesus offers and merciful hearts to extend the hope of a second chance to everyone who enters the church.

Suggested Overnight Retreat Schedule

If you'd like to extend this event into an overnight retreat, use this schedule as a starting point.

Day	Time	Activities	Supplies
Friday	7:00 p.m.-7:45 p.m.	Bread Line	
		Horse Races	Paper, markers, tape, children's toys as "horses"
	7:45 p.m.-10:15 p.m.	*Seabiscuit*	Movie: *Seabiscuit*, DVD player or VCR, TV
	10:15 p.m.-10:30 p.m.	Snacks	
	10:30 p.m.-11:30 p.m.	Free time	
	Midnight	Lights out	
Saturday	8:00 a.m.-8:30 a.m.	Devotion	
	8:30 a.m.-9:00 a.m.	Breakfast	
	9:00 a.m.-9:30 a.m.	*Human Resources*	Bibles, marker, "Human Resources" handout (p. 75), pens or pencils
	9:30 a.m.-noon	Games or group activities	
	Noon-1:00 p.m.	Lunch	
	1:00 p.m.-3:00 p.m.	Free time	
	3:00 p.m.-3:30 p.m.	*Discussion*	
		Eternal Bandages	Bible, adhesive bandages, markers
		Get Out of Jail Free	Bible, "Get Out of Jail Free" handout (p. 76), scissors
	3:30 p.m.-5:00 p.m.	Free time	
	5:00 p.m.-6:00 p.m.	Dinner	
	6:00 p.m.-7:30 p.m.	Worship and prayer	
	7:30 p.m.-8:00 p.m.	Pack and leave	

Human Resources

Human Resources: For internal use only

Position: Senior Pastor

Qualifications: A righteous man or woman with pastoral experience and a heart for God

Candidate 1:

Convicted of murder. Hiding from justice in the wilderness. (See Exodus 2:10-15.)

Candidate 2:

Top of his class in seminary. Diligently fights heresy in the church. (See Acts 7:54–8:3.)

Candidate 3:

Talented musician, but prone to promiscuity. (See 2 Samuel 11:1-4.)

Candidate 4:

A loudmouth who cracks under pressure. (See Luke 22:54-62.)

Candidate 5:

A homeless man sentenced to life in prison. (See Matthew 14:1-10.)

Candidate 6:

A successful, law-abiding young man. (See Luke 18:18-25.)

Candidate 7:

A cowardly farmer. (See Judges 6:11-16.)

Candidate 8:

Fudges the truth and runs a bordello. (See Joshua 2:1-6.)

Candidate 9:

Sons of the High Priest, raised in the church. (See 1 Samuel 2:12-17.)

Candidate 10:

A child prone to fits of anger. (See John 2:13-17.)

Human Resources

Get Out of Jail Free

"For there is no difference between Jew and Gentile—the same

This Card
May Be Kept
Until Needed
or Sold

Get Out of Jail Free

who call on him, for, "Everyone who calls on the name of the Lord

will be saved" " (Romans 10:12-13).

Lord is Lord of all and richly blesses all

"For there is no difference between Jew and Gentile—the same

This Card
May Be Kept
Until Needed
or Sold

Get Out of Jail Free

who call on him, for, "Everyone who calls on the name of the Lord

will be saved" " (Romans 10:12-13).

Lord is Lord of all and richly blesses all

"For there is no difference between Jew and Gentile—the same

This Card
May Be Kept
Until Needed
or Sold

Get Out of Jail Free

who call on him, for, "Everyone who calls on the name of the Lord

will be saved" " (Romans 10:12-13).

Lord is Lord of all and richly blesses all

"For there is no difference between Jew and Gentile—the same

This Card
May Be Kept
Until Needed
or Sold

Get Out of Jail Free

who call on him, for, "Everyone who calls on the name of the Lord

will be saved" " (Romans 10:12-13).

Lord is Lord of all and richly blesses all

"For there is no difference between Jew and Gentile—the same

This Card
May Be Kept
Until Needed
or Sold

Get Out of Jail Free

who call on him, for, "Everyone who calls on the name of the Lord

will be saved" " (Romans 10:12-13).

Lord is Lord of all and richly blesses all

"For there is no difference between Jew and Gentile—the same

This Card
May Be Kept
Until Needed
or Sold

Get Out of Jail Free

who call on him, for, "Everyone who calls on the name of the Lord

will be saved" " (Romans 10:12-13).

Lord is Lord of all and richly blesses all

"For there is no difference between Jew and Gentile—the same

This Card
May Be Kept
Until Needed
or Sold

Get Out of Jail Free

who call on him, for, "Everyone who calls on the name of the Lord

will be saved" " (Romans 10:12-13).

Lord is Lord of all and richly blesses all

"For there is no difference between Jew and Gentile—the same

This Card
May Be Kept
Until Needed
or Sold

Get Out of Jail Free

who call on him, for, "Everyone who calls on the name of the Lord

will be saved" " (Romans 10:12-13).

Lord is Lord of all and richly blesses all

Movie:

Signs
(Touchstone, 2002)

Rating:

PG-13 for some frightening moments

The Props

☐ *Bibles*
☐ *movie: Signs*
☐ *DVD player or VCR*
☐ *TV or video projector*
☐ *aluminum foil*
☐ *"Increasing Faith Stations" handout (p. 83)*
☐ *scissors*
☐ *bucket of modeling dough*
☐ *2 tables*
☐ *several clocks and watches with hands that can be adjusted by winding*
☐ *colored construction paper*
☐ *bowl of ice cubes*
☐ *several flashlights*
☐ *several newspapers*
☐ *cardboard*
☐ *fabric*
☐ *glue*
☐ *plywood*
☐ *saw*
☐ *drill*
☐ *bowl of mustard seeds*

Can You Read the Signs?
Getting a Grip on Faith

The Pitch

Signs delivers some genuine chills while asking universal questions about faith and coincidence. After surviving this "alien invasion," your young people will understand the relationship between a faith they can't see and their physical, everyday life.

Favorite Quote

"Though you have not seen him, you love him; and even though you do not see him now, you believe in him and are filled with an inexpressible and glorious joy" (1 Peter 1:8).

More Quotables: Luke 17:5-6; John 20:24-29; 2 Corinthians 5:7; 1 Peter 1:8-9

Suggested Schedule

Section	Activities	Time	Supplies
The Red Carpet	*2 UFO or Not 2 UFO*	25-30 minutes	Aluminum foil
The Production	*Signs*	105 minutes	Movie: *Signs*, DVD player or VCR, TV
Postproduction	*Discussion*	15-20 minutes	Bible
	Increasing Faith Stations	35-40 minutes	Bible, "Increasing Faith Stations" handout (p. 83), scissors, bucket of modeling dough, tables, clocks and watches, construction paper, bowl of ice cubes, flashlights, newspapers
Word of Mouth	*Doubting Thomas*	5-10 minutes	Bible, cardboard, fabric, glue, scissors, plywood, saw, drill, bowl of mustard seeds

Take 78
Blockbuster Movie Events

Movie Review

Signs centers on Graham Hess (Mel Gibson), a former pastor who lost his faith in God after the accidental death of his wife. An intergalactic confrontation with unfriendly invading aliens lends meaning to the strange coincidences that swirled around his wife's death.

Faith is always a difficult subject to discuss because you can't see it or touch it or place it on a table to examine. Despite its ethereal quality, it's the fuel that drives a person's relationship with God. *Signs* does an excellent job of placing some skin over this spiritual subject. (It lacks an airtight script, though: The aliens travel through space but can't open doors? They attack a planet that's more than 90 percent "poisonous" water?) The movie seems to question the notion that life is random; instead, God is controlling things so they work out for the good. This experience will bring alive the abstract concept of faith and will help your young people connect faith with tangible, everyday experiences.

Pastoral Guidance

Signs is one of the least offensive "scary" movies ever committed to film, and it largely chooses tension over gore. The film includes only a half-dozen profanities, almost exclusively in two prominent scenes: when Graham and Merrill Hess (Joaquin Phoenix) run around the house (14:30–15:00) and when a girl gives impromptu confession to Graham (28:45–29:15). These scenes actually show character traits that add to the plot while providing some necessary laughs.

Be sensitive to any students who have experienced the death of loved ones; the scenes depicting Graham's wife's death are emotionally intense. (See page 5 for more details or visit www.screenit.com for a detailed list of the film's content.)

Preproduction

Set up a movie viewing area with the TV or projector and VCR or DVD player. Have the movie set up and ready to go.

The "Increasing Faith" stations require some careful preparation. First you'll need to designate six different areas within your meeting space for the stations. The stations should be easy to find but far enough apart so that several people can enjoy each station simultaneously without interfering with others. Photocopy the "Increasing Faith Stations" handout (p. 83), cut apart the instructions, and place each station's instructions prominently in one of the six designated areas.
- *For the "Chair" station, place a bucket of modeling dough on a table.*
- *For the "Clock" station, set a few clocks and watches with hands that can be adjusted by winding.*
- *For the "Airplane" station, place a stack of multicolored sheets of construction paper on the floor.*
- *For the "Antarctic" station, place a bowl of ice cubes on a small table.*

PRODUCTION TIP

If possible, recruit six adult volunteers to provide assistance at each "Increasing Faith" station. These volunteers can direct young people to the station's directions, as well as rearrange any supplies as students move in and out of the stations.

- *For the "Flashlight" station, place several flashlights next to the entrance of a dark, enclosed space such as a closet or office.*
- *For the "News" station, spread several newspapers and set out pairs of scissors.*

Create a "Jesus" figure *without* a distinguishable face—one that you've cut out of cardboard; a mannequin; or a silhouette, cut out of butcher paper and taped to a wall, for example. Just be sure the figure is life-sized. Cut a robe from fabric, and secure it to the figure. Most importantly, give Jesus "hands." Cut hand shapes out of plywood, then drill a ¾-inch to 1-inch hole through each wrist. Affix the hands to the proper position on the Jesus figure. Your teenagers will be sticking their fingers through the "nail prints" for a moving experience. Place a bowl of mustard seeds at the figure's feet.

> **PRODUCTION TIP**
>
> When creating the plywood hands, don't feel the need to cut around each finger. It's fine to draw the fingers and other characteristics of hands on the plywood.

> **PRODUCTION TIP**
>
> If you're "constructionally challenged," create Jesus' "hands" from clay. Be sure to poke a hole through the clay in the wrist area.

Bonus Swag

Use these ideas to produce even more of the movie's ambience throughout this event.

- *Place 2x4s and plywood around the room with hammers and cups and nails as if preparing for the alien assault.*
- *Place half-filled glasses of water on every available surface.*
- *Set up a strong work light outside one of the windows so it shines inside the room like an alien intrusion.*
- *Set out a baby monitor that emits random noises.*
- *Hang an alien mask so it peeks in a window from outside.*
- *Tape to the walls tabloid stories about crop circles and patterns.*

WEB SITE NOTE: *Be sure to check out www.group.com/blockbusterevents for great resources to promote and plan these events!*

The Red Carpet

As participants arrive, hand each a sheet of aluminum foil. Instruct teenagers to mold a hat from the foil to protect their brain waves from aliens.

> **SPECIAL EFFECTS**
>
> Play the creepy audio from the *Signs* DVD menu as participants enter.

2 UFO or Not 2 UFO

Once everyone is seated, say: **Before we get started, I have one question: Who believes in the existence of alien life forms? Raise your hand. Don't be shy!**

Ask the people who raise their hands to form a group, and have everyone else form another group.

Explain that you're going to pose several questions and that groups will debate opposing viewpoints as to the answers. Each group will choose someone to debate the first question, then a second debater to tackle the second question, and so on until all questions have been debated or all participants have had a chance to debate.

> **PRODUCTION TIP**
>
> As a precaution against grossly uneven groups, have some adult volunteers ready to argue either side (though perhaps they should prepare to fight in defense of the existence of extraterrestrials).

When everyone understands, pose the following topics one by one. Allow each side to argue its position for one minute. The topics are as follows:

- *Why do you believe spaceships do or do not exist?*
- *Does "area 51" exist?*
- *Where did the pyramids in Egypt come from? Who built them?*
- *Why would God create life only on earth?*
- *What does the Bible say about aliens?*
- *Is the testimony of "alien abductees" credible?*

- *Do extraterrestrial life forms exist?*
- *How do you explain the disappearances in the Bermuda Triangle?*

Say: **This debate could go on indefinitely because neither side can *prove* its position. Both sides operate from a position of faith.**

Ask: • *How is this similar to Christianity?*

Say: In 2 Corinthians 5:7, Paul wrote, "We live by faith, not by sight." Be thinking about the issue of faith as you watch tonight's exciting encounter with aliens in *Signs*.

The Production—*Signs*

Gather everyone around the TV to watch the movie. Start the film, sit back, relax, and enjoy!

Postproduction

Discussion

After the movie, allow everyone a five-minute break. When everyone has returned, have teenagers form groups of four or five to discuss the following questions:

- *Do you see life as a series of signs with purpose or as random coincidences? Why?*
- *How does your perspective impact your ability to have faith in a God you can't see?*
- *What are some reasons people give for not having faith in God?*
- *Why do you think God doesn't simply appear in person to the world so there wouldn't be any need for faith?*

Say: **Having faith can be difficult because circumstances and crises and questions constantly arise to cast doubt upon your beliefs. Plus we experience life-changing moments when we learn that something we believed in is not, after all, real.**

Ask: • *How did you feel when you learned that Santa Claus wasn't real?*
- *What else have you had faith in that didn't stand up over time?*
- *How do you decide what you will believe in?*
- *What kinds of things test your faith in God?*
- *How do you typically address these doubts?*

Read aloud Luke 17:5-6. Say: **One great thing about God is that he doesn't turn a cold shoulder to us. We can ask for faith, and it's so powerful that the faithful can serve God in miraculous ways.**

Increasing Faith Stations

Say: **Faith can be hard to grasp because we don't stop to connect it to our everyday lives, so we're going to do just that.** Point out each "Increasing Faith" station around the room, and say: **Each station represents something in everyday life in which you have faith and then explores how that relates to faith in your spiritual life.**

Explain the directions for each station, using page 83 as a guide. Then say: **You are welcome to do the stations in any order and at any pace. If you find a crowd at one station, try another one first. Instructions for each station are posted in case you forget what to do. There are only two rules: (1) Only one person at a time should be in the (dark area such as a closet) at the "Flashlight" station, and (2) you must remain silent. This is a time for personal experience and reflection. Please don't ruin someone else's experience by talking. When you finish, please find a seat and wait quietly.**

Plan for students to experience the stations for about 30 minutes. Prompt them when five minutes remains so they can finish. Then gather everyone together, and ask a volunteer to read aloud 1 Peter 1:8-9.

Say: **My prayer is that you've connected with God and increased your faith. When you see a flashlight or chair during the next week, you will be filled with joy at the fact that you can place complete faith in our God who will never disappoint.**

> ## SPECIAL EFFECTS
>
> Play the clip from *The Santa Clause 2* (G), located from 53:30–56:00, where Carol tells Scott that she lost her capacity to believe when she learned that Santa Claus didn't really exist.

> ## SPECIAL EFFECTS
>
> Play mellow background music while students experience the "Increasing Faith" stations.

Word of Mouth

Doubting Thomas

Say: Faith is an amazing thing that can help you throughout life. Jesus said that those who don't see him are blessed for having tremendous faith.

Have someone read aloud John 20:24-29. Say: **Jesus was human. He knows how hard it is to believe in things you can't see. That's why we can pray to him for faith, and that's why he understands when we ask for assurance that he's there and cares.**

Show youth the Jesus figure you set up before the event.

Say: For the rest of our time, you are free to pray at Jesus' feet, asking him to increase your faith and bless you because you have not seen him. This Jesus even has holes in his hands so you can feel where the nails pierced him.

When you finish praying, take a mustard seed from the bowl at his feet. Keep it as a reminder of how it takes only a small seed to grow into a mighty tree of faith.

As teenagers finish praying, quietly remind them to take home any items they created at the stations.

Suggested Overnight Retreat Schedule

If you'd like to extend this event into an overnight retreat, use this schedule as a starting point.

Day	Time	Activities	Supplies
Friday	7:00 p.m.-7:30 p.m.	*2 UFO or Not 2 UFO*	Aluminum foil
	7:30 p.m.-9:15 p.m.	*Signs*	Movie: *Signs*, DVD player or VCR, TV
	9:15 p.m.-9:35 p.m.	*Discussion*	Bible
	9:35 p.m.-10:00 p.m.	Snacks	
	10:00 p.m.-11:30 p.m.	Free time	
	Midnight	Lights out	
Saturday	8:00 a.m.-8:30 a.m.	Devotion	
	8:30 a.m.-9:00 a.m.	Breakfast	
	9:00 a.m.-9:40 a.m.	*Increasing Faith Stations*	Bible, "Increasing Faith Stations" handout (p. 83), scissors, bucket of modeling dough, tables, clocks and watches, construction paper, bowl of ice cubes, flashlights, newspaper
	9:40 a.m.-noon	Games or group activities	
	Noon-1:00 p.m.	Lunch	
	1:00 p.m.-3:00 p.m.	Free time	
	3:00 p.m.-3:15 p.m.	*Doubting Thomas*	Bible, cardboard, fabric, glue, scissors, plywood, saw, drill, bowl of mustard seeds
	3:15 p.m.-5:00 p.m.	Free time	
	5:00 p.m.-6:00 p.m.	Dinner	
	6:00 p.m.-7:30 p.m.	Worship and prayer	
	7:30 p.m.-8:00 p.m.	Pack and leave	

Increasing Faith Stations

- **The Chair**—Every day we put faith in our chairs to hold us up when we sit. Mold a chair from modeling dough, and pray for faith that God will catch you when you fall. Leave your chair at the station when you finish.

- **The Clock**—When we see a clock, we trust that it's telling the correct time. As you spin the hands of this clock around, pray for increased faith that God is in control of everything that's going on at all times.

- **The Airplane**—People put their faith in an airplane's ability to fly and land safely. Make a paper airplane from the construction paper, praying for increased faith in God's guidance. Pray that God will take you where you need to go. Leave your plane at the station when you finish.

- **The Antarctic**—We believe in the existence of places we've never seen firsthand such as Antarctica. Take a piece of "Antarctic ice" and grip it tightly. As it melts, pray for faith that the Creator is still intimately involved in building the Church just as he built the world.

- **The Flashlight**—We have faith that power will be available to ignite lights. When the space is free, take the flashlight with you. As the darkness surrounds you, pray for God to increase your faith in Jesus as the light of the world. When you finish, turn on the flashlight and witness the light chasing away the darkness. (Please, only one person in the darkness at a time.)

- **The News**—Many people believe that newspapers print the truth. Cut out words that relate to your life, praying for faith in the Bible was God's perfect Word of truth that relates to your life today.

Movie:

Spider-Man 2
(Columbia, 2004)

Rating:

PG-13 for stylized action violence

The Props

- [ ] *Bibles*
- [ ] *movie: Spider-Man 2*
- [ ] *DVD player or VCR*
- [ ] *TV or video projector*
- [ ] *T-shirts*
- [ ] *art supplies such as colored permanent markers, sequins, glue, glitter, ribbon, sparkles, puffy paint, construction paper, and pipe cleaners*
- [ ] *cardboard*
- [ ] *scissors*
- [ ] *aluminum foil*
- [ ] *2 sheets tied into togas*
- [ ] *2 chairs*
- [ ] *tape*
- [ ] *newsprint*
- [ ] *large city map*
- [ ] *straight pins with colored heads*

Rise of the Super Hero:
Laying Down Your Life in Service

The Pitch

Spider-Man 2 presents one of our most beloved comic-book heroes as a shining example of someone who lays down his life to serve others. After experiencing this event, young people will be excited about serving others and will have a clear mission for transforming a hurting world through acts rooted in the gospel.

Favorite Quote

"My command is this: Love each other as I have loved you. Greater love has no one than this, that he lay down his life for his friends" (John 15:12-13).

More Quotables: John 13:4-5,14-15; Romans 12

Suggested Schedule

Section	Activities	Time	Supplies
The Red Carpet	*I Am a Hero*	10-15 minutes	T-Shirts, art supplies
The Production	*Spider-Man 2*	120 minutes	Movie: *Spider-Man 2*, DVD player or VCR, TV
Postproduction	*Discussion*	10-15 minutes	
	One Willing Monk	15-20 minutes	Bibles, cardboard, scissors, aluminum foil, togas, chairs
	Heroic Plans	25-30 minutes	Bibles, newsprint, tape, marker
Word of Mouth	*Mapping Our Heroics*	5-10 minutes	City map, tape, straight pins

Movie Review

Peter Parker (Tobey Maguire) returns as your friendly neighborhood Spider-Man in this thrilling sequel. Times are tough for the web-slinger. He's broke; failing his classes; facing eviction; and certain to lose his true love, Mary Jane Watson (Kirsten Dunst), to an astronaut. Peter decides to hang up his costume for good, ignoring the need around him and focusing on making himself happy. Forced out of retirement by an out-of-control Doc Ock (Alfred Molina), Peter fights for the lives of his loved ones, masses of innocent people in New York City, and himself.

Spider-Man 2 improves upon the original in every way possible, most notably by inspiring the audience to become better people. Peter Parker stands in stark contrast to a world that constantly encourages people to look out for number one. Christ died so that we might live; Spider-Man fights to protect the innocent (and not so blameless) at the expense of his own personal happiness. This event will energize your youth with a vision for changing their community. And because of the ubiquitous presence of Spider-Man in our culture, your students constantly will be reminded of their desire to serve every time they see the web-slinger's face.

Pastoral Guidance

The only offensive material in *Spider-Man 2* is the extensive violence. When Doc Ock awakens in a hospital, he murders several doctors and nurses in horror-style fashion. His battles with Spidey, in hyper-realistic comic-book style, are quite brutal. (See page 5 for more details or visit www.screenit.com for a detailed list of the film's content.)

Preproduction

Set up a movie viewing area with the TV or projector and VCR or DVD player. Have the movie set up and ready to go.

Announce repeatedly to your teenagers that they should bring an old or secondhand T-shirt to the event to decorate. Then bring extra T-shirts to accommodate students who don't bring them.

Position a large table in one corner of your meeting area, leaving plenty of room around all four sides so people can approach it from any direction. Place art supplies such as colored permanent markers, sequins, glue, glitter, ribbon, sparkles, puffy paint, construction paper, pipe cleaners, fabric, scissors, and extra T-shirts on the table.

Cut out two sword shapes from cardboard, and cover them with aluminum foil. Write the words from John 15:12-13 on the swords.

Recruit an adult volunteer to help with the "One Willing Monk" drama. This person should help two student actors don togas over their street clothes and give the cardboard swords to the other actors. The volunteer also will explain that the beginning of the skit gets a lot of laughs but then ends very seriously, so it's not appropriate for them to ham it up once the gladiators enter the drama. The adult volunteer should let the "monk" know that

Take 85
Blockbuster
Movie Events

he will die and should simply fall down dead instead of performing a drawn out, hokey death scene. Finally, the adult volunteer should place two chairs in the center of the "stage" for the monk and Aquilla to sit on at the "coliseum" and should keep the gladiators off the stage until they're called into the scene.

Tape a large piece of newsprint to a wall for the "Heroic Plans" activity.

Tape to a wall the largest map of your city you can find. Position the straight pins nearby.

Bonus Swag

Use these ideas to produce even more of the movie's ambience throughout this event.

SPECIAL EFFECTS

Invite youth ministry groups from area churches to this event. With "super heroes" from all over your town gathered together, teenagers will think of amazing ideas for serving others. You'll also galvanize area youth workers to work together. Finally, your young people will gain comfort and a sense of mission when they realize their town is full of Christian heroes.

- *Deck out the meeting room with plenty of fake spider webs and plastic spiders hanging from the ceiling and clinging to the corners.*
- *Cover one wall with black butcher paper, and cut a massive skyline from it. This "city silhouette" will serve as a beautiful backdrop for the event.*
- *Recruit an adult volunteer to act as a photographer, taking pictures for the newspaper's society section.*

WEB SITE NOTE: *Be sure to check out www.group.com/blockbusterevents for great resources to promote and plan these events!*

The Red Carpet
I Am a Hero

After everyone has arrived, say: **Welcome to our very first convention of** [your town] **Super Heroes! Each**

and every one of you has an amazing power like X-ray vision, invisibility, impeccable fashion sense, or speedy computer skills. As you know, every super hero has a costume, so you need to make yours!

SPECIAL EFFECTS

Have the *Spider-Man 2* movie soundtrack playing while teenagers create their super hero costumes.

Explain that youth are going to use T-shirts and art supplies to create their super hero costumes; while they work, they should figure out what their super powers are and what their super hero name is. Point out the table of art supplies and extra T-shirts, and encourage teenagers to be creative. Give students about seven minutes to work.

After about seven minutes, instruct teenagers to put on their costumes for a fashion show. Have everyone stand in a large circle so each super hero can be seen. Explain that each person should take a turn stepping forward, telling his or her super hero name, and explaining his or her super power. Afterward, applaud all the super heroes. Then say:

We're going to see what it means to be a super hero by watching the story of Peter Parker, one of our greatest costumed crusaders. As we watch his adventures, remember the immortal words of the greatest hero in history: Jesus said in John 15:12-13, "My command is this: Love each other as I have loved you. Greater love has no one than this, that he lay down his life for his friends" Let's watch how Spider-Man exemplifies this command.

The Production— *Spider Man 2*

Gather everyone around the TV to watch the movie. Start the film, sit back, relax, and enjoy!

Postproduction
Discussion

When the movie ends, allow a five-minute break. When everyone returns, ask:

- *How would you have felt about being a super hero if you'd faced the problems Peter faced?*
- *Do you think Peter should have quit being Spider-Man? Why or why not?*
- *What leads you to think of yourself over other people? What leads you to think of others' needs?*

Say: **Service to others is what powers the heart of a hero. It's rarely easy to put others first, as Peter Parker discovered, but history is filled with examples of people who impacted the world by doing just that.**

One Willing Monk

Ask for four volunteers to help with this activity. Have the adult volunteer take the volunteers aside and quietly prepare them for their roles in the "One Willing Monk" skit. Meanwhile, say: **We're going to see a drama about one person's heroism, but our four volunteers don't know the story or any lines. I'm going to read the drama, and they will act out what I say. Pay attention, because the crowd also will get involved.**

When the volunteers are ready, read the following narrative with pauses to allow the actors to respond to their roles.

Aquilla stood in the town square, minding her own business, when a monk approached her. The monk tapped her on the shoulder. He tapped her harder. Aquilla turned around. The monk said, "Could you please tell me what the bell means?" Aquilla looked the monk up and down. She walked around him. She looked very concerned. "You're not from around here," she said. The monk modeled his robes. He twirled for her. "I'm a monk," he said. Aquilla rolled her eyes. She rolled them larger. She said, "I never would've guessed." Aquilla

If you invited area youth groups, your TV likely will not accommodate the additional viewers. You can project the movie on the side of a large building with a video projector and speakers.

continued, "The bell means it's time to go to the coliseum." The monk got excited. He got more excited. He jumped up and down. "Can I go with you?" he asked. Aquilla nodded. "Sure," she said.

Aquilla and the monk walked slowly. More slowly. So slowly that they looked like they were walking in place. Aquilla asked, "Are you here for a monk convention?" The monk laughed. He took a huge breath and laughed louder. Then he stopped laughing and said, "I read a book about Rome. When I finished, I knew I had to come. It was as if Jesus himself told me to come."

Aquilla gasped. She gasped again. "Ixnay on the Esus-jay. He's not too popular round here," she said. The monk looked confused. He asked, "Why?"

Aquilla snorted. Louder. Like a horse. She said, "People don't like being told what to do."

The monk chuckled. "People say Rome's too big for one person, but my God is big enough to use me here."

Aquilla stopped and held out her arms wide. Not that wide. "Here we are!" They entered the coliseum, found their seats, and sat down.

Two gladiators marched out to the center of the coliseum. They raised their swords to the crowd. The crowd clapped and cheered. When the crowd quieted down, the monk said to Aquilla, "Those are gladiators! They won't kill each other, will they?"

Aquilla looked at the monk as if he'd grown two heads. "It's not called 'fight to the death' for nothing." The monk leapt to his feet and shouted, "This is wrong!"

The gladiators circled each other, preparing to fight. The crowd cheered with approval. The monk jumped into the ring with the gladiators. He stood in front of one gladiator and pleaded with him. "Please! In the name of Jesus Christ who died for you, you don't have to do this!" The gladiator shoved the monk to the ground.

The monk jumped up and got in front of the second gladiator. "Listen to me! In the name of Jesus Christ who died for you, you don't have to do this!" The gladiator pushed the monk away and shouted, "Get out of here!"

The two gladiators approached each other, swords raised. The monk leapt to his feet, shouting, "In the name of Jesus Christ our Lord who died for you, you don't have to do this!" The monk put himself between the two gladiators. One of the gladiators stabbed the monk with his sword.

The gladiators slowly backed away as the monk grabbed his

wound. The monk fell to the ground. With his last breath, he gasped, "In the name of Jesus Christ who died for you, you don't have to do this." With that, he died.

After the monk died, the gladiators slowly left the arena. Next some crowd members quietly got up and left. Then the emperor and his court left, followed by more spectators. . .until the coliseum was completely empty. That was the final gladiator fight ever held in the city of Rome.

(Narrative adapted from *Ultimate Skits* © 2002 by Bryan Belknap. Reprinted by permission of Group Publishing, Inc., P.O. Box 481, Loveland, CO 80539.)

Lead the audience in applauding the actors. Instruct teenagers to turn to a partner to discuss these questions:
- *How did this skit make you feel?*
- *Do you think you could be like the monk? Why or why not?*

Ask pairs to read John 13:4-5, 14-15 and discuss the following questions:
- *Have you ever served someone and been disappointed with the results? If so, what happened?*
- *What, if anything, do our expectations have to do with whether our service is successful?*
- *What are some practical ways to keep a heavenly perspective when serving on earth?*

Say: **Telemechus, the monk portrayed in this drama, provides a powerful example of what it means to be a servant. I don't mean that we should die when we serve, but we can help people and stand up for justice without knowing the outcome. We might never see the impact of our service in this life, but we trust that God will use it for good. That's why we follow the servant example of our hero Jesus Christ.**

Heroic Plans

Have teenagers form groups of six. Say: **Let's face it: Captain Couch Potato never makes the news because he never leaves the house! We're going to form some super hero teams called Justice Brigades and figure out some practical ways to make a positive difference in our community.**

To help give you some context for what it means to be a servant hero, we're going to use Paul's description from Romans 12. Take the next five minutes to read the chapter and discuss how it connects to serving others.

Give students five minutes to read and discuss. Say: **Now based on what you discussed, your Justice Brigade will spend time coming up with an idea for living out Romans 12 right here in our community. Push one another to be as creative as possible. No idea is too outrageous for super heroes! Agree on an area of need in the community, and create a hands-on method for tackling it. After 10 minutes, we'll share our ideas.**

Allow the Justice Brigades to spread out and brainstorm. Circulate among the groups, helping those that seem stuck. After 10 minutes, have a representative from each group share the heroic ideas. As groups share, write their ideas on the sheet of newsprint you posted before the event. After every group has shared, have the entire group decide upon one idea to focus on collectively. Then ask:
- *How does this idea share the love of Jesus Christ?*
- *How does this idea meet people's needs?*
- *What must we do to put this plan into action?*

Say: **This town is never going to be the same! Spider-Man may have the cool powers, but we are the people who can truly make a difference. We can ease suffering and share the love of Christ.**

Word of Mouth
Mapping Our Heroics

Point out the map of your town, which you posted before the event. Say: **This is a map of our town, and we all have an important part to play in spreading the light of Jesus Christ through it.**

Have each person place on the map a straight pin that represents the location of his or her home. Afterward, say: **Serving others can sometimes seem overwhelming, but look at this map. Heroes live all over our town. Look around this room. It's filled with other super heroes—all with unique powers, all ready and willing to fight alongside you for justice. You are not alone!**

Close with prayer, asking God to inspire the group to fulfill its call to service for God's glory.

Suggested Overnight Retreat Schedule

If you'd like to extend this event into an overnight retreat, use this schedule as a starting point.

Day	Time	Activities	Supplies
Friday	7:00 p.m.-7:45 p.m.	*I Am a Hero*	T-shirts, art supplies
	7:45 p.m.-9:45 p.m.	*Spider-Man 2*	Movie: *Spider-Man 2*, DVD player or VCR, TV
	9:45 p.m.-10:00 p.m.	*Discussion*	
	10:00 p.m.-10:30 p.m.	Snacks	
	10:30 p.m.-11:30 p.m.	Free time	
	Midnight	Lights out	
Saturday	8:00 a.m.-8:30 a.m.	Devotion	
	8:30 a.m.-9:00 a.m.	Breakfast	
	9:00 a.m.-10:00 a.m.	*One Willing Monk* *Heroic Plans*	Bibles, cardboard, scissors, aluminum foil, togas, chairs Bibles, newsprint, tape, marker
	10:00 a.m.-noon	Games or group activities	
	Noon-1:00 p.m.	Lunch	
	1:00 p.m.-3:00 p.m.	Free time	
	3:00 p.m.-4:00 p.m.	Heroic Plan Presentation	
	4:00 p.m.-5:00 p.m.	Free time	
	5:00 p.m.-6:00 p.m.	Dinner	
	6:00 p.m.-7:30 p.m.	Worship and prayer *Mapping Our Heroics*	 City map, tape, straight pins
	7:30 p.m.-8:00 p.m.	Pack and leave	

Movie:

A Walk to Remember
(Warner Brothers, 2003)

Rating:

PG for thematic elements, language, and some sensual material

The Props

- [ ] *Bibles*
- [ ] *movie:*
  A Walk to Remember
- [ ] *DVD player or VCR*
- [ ] *TV or video projector*
- [ ] *enough photocopies of the "Mating Game" handout (p. 95) that each person will receive a card*
- [ ] *pens or pencils*
- [ ] *scissors*
- [ ] *newsprint*
- [ ] *marker*
- [ ] *tape*
- [ ] *2 Lego building blocks for each person*
- [ ] *1 "Building the Perfect Mate/Love Letter" handout (p.96) for each person*
- [ ] *several hammers and screwdrivers*
- [ ] *super glue*

Walking the Walk:
Saving Sex for Marriage

The Pitch

A Walk to Remember is Hollywood's most sympathetic and positive portrayal of a Christian on film, showcasing the brave decision of a young woman to remain sexually pure. Through this movie event, your young people will build a solid foundation for lasting romantic love that saves sexual intercourse until marriage.

Favorite Quote

"Flee from sexual immorality. All other sins a man commits are outside his body, but he who sins sexually sins against his own body" (1 Corinthians 6:18).

More Quotables: Matthew 6:25-33; 19:4-6; 1 Corinthians 13; Psalm 40:1-3

Suggested Schedule

Section	Activities	Time	Supplies
The Red Carpet	*The Mating Game*	10-15 minutes	"The Mating Game" handout (p. 95), scissors, pens or pencils
The Production	*A Walk to Remember*	105 minutes	Movie: *A Walk to Remember*, DVD player or VCR, TV
Postproduction	*Building the Perfect Spouse*	30-35 minutes	Bibles, newsprint, marker, tape, "Building the Perfect Mate" handout (p. 96), pens or pencils
	Leggo My Spouse, Oh!	30-35 minutes	Bible, Lego blocks, super glue, hammers, screwdrivers
Word of Mouth	*Love Letter*	15-20 minutes	"Love Letter" handout (p. 96), pens or pencils

Movie Review

A Walk to Remember stars Mandy Moore as goody-two-shoes Christian Jamie Sullivan. Resident bad boy Landon Carter (Shane West) becomes enmeshed inside Jamie's sphere of influence through the school play and required community service. As Landon hangs around Jamie, he realizes there's much more to the pastor's daughter than her trademark sweater. As Landon softens, Jamie finds a loving, caring, honorable young man lurking under the tough exterior. Though no one thought it possible, a love blossoms between the pair—a love that teaches everyone the true meaning of commitment and romance.

You probably won't find a more sympathetic portrayal of a Christian teen in modern film (though the theology isn't airtight, as Jamie claims that God wants her to "be happy.") While other teen films glamorize hormone-crazed sex addicts, *A Walk to Remember* treats teenagers with respect. Your young people not only will see the proper way to conduct themselves sexually, but also will see that their dating relationships set the tone for their future marriages. By learning the proper respect for intercourse and the opposite sex, your young people will leave this experience with a passion for honoring God and their future spouse.

Pastoral Guidance

A Walk to Remember contains a dozen scattered profanities and sexual situations—all limited to sexual comments and making out. (Remember, it's a teen romance.) Also, since the main character dies (sorry to spoil the movie for you), any of your young people dealing with debilitating illnesses or with grief may have strong emotional reactions. (See page 5 for more details or visit www.screenit.com for a detailed list of the film's content.)

Preproduction

Set up a movie viewing area with the TV or projector and VCR or DVD player. Have the movie set up and ready to go.

Make enough copies of "The Mating Game" handout (p. 95) for each participant to receive one square. Cut apart the squares, and number the back of each square consecutively. You'll choose a number during the event, and the person with that card will be your contestant.

Arrange for adult volunteers to dress and act as ushers, walking each entrant to a seat in the meeting area.

Tape two sheets of newsprint where the entire group will be able to see them, but keep them hidden until the appropriate time. Draw the bathroom door symbol for a female on one sheet, and draw the bathroom door symbol for a male on the other. Leave plenty of room for writing a list on each sheet.

Place a table in one area of your meeting space where you can spread out plenty of Lego blocks, bottles of super glue, hammers, and screwdrivers.

Bonus Swag

Use these ideas to produce even more of the movie's ambience throughout this event.

- *Decorate your meeting room as if you're preparing to celebrate a wedding ceremony. Borrow floral arrangements from around the church, light a unity candle, and roll a white runner down the center of the space or the entrance to your meeting area.*
- *Ask an adult volunteer to act as a "wedding photographer" for the event.*
- *Create a banner that says "just married," and hang aluminum cans from it like a decorated car.*
- *Provide a small wedding cake, complete with the plastic groom and bride figures on top.*
- *Provide small bottles of bubbles like the ones family and friends blow on a newly married couple as they exit the church.*

WEB SITE NOTE: *Be sure to check out www.group.com/blockbusterevents for great resources to promote and plan these events!*

The Red Carpet

As your "wedding guests" enter, hand each a card from the "Mating Game" handout (p. 95) and a pen or pencil. Instruct each entrant to answer the questions on the "wedding program." Have your adult volunteers escort each person into the meeting area.

Once everyone is seated, say: **Welcome to the wedding of Landon and Jamie! They are so happy you could join them for this special event. Before we watch the video about how they met and fell in love, they've devised a fun way for two of you to leave as happy and in love as they are.**

The Mating Game

Say: **Each of you should have answered the questions you received when you came in. Now look on the back of your cards. Would the person who has number** [choose a number] **come join me?**

[Contestant] **is the lucky person who will find** [his or her] **perfect mate. Look at your answers to the three**

> **SPECIAL EFFECTS**
>
> While your guests find their seats, have romantic music such as the *Walk to Remember* soundtrack playing.

questions on your card. We're going to ask [contestant] what [he or she] wrote. If you wrote the same answer, please stand up and remain standing as long as you wrote the same answers as [contestant].

Have your contestant read aloud the answer to the first question, and ask all persons of the opposite sex who answered the same way stand up. Then have your contestant read aloud the answer to the second question. From the group already standing, have those who answered differently sit down. Repeat the process for the final question.

If no one answered all three questions the same as your contestant, choose the person with the most identical answers. If more than one person answered all three questions the same as your contestant, break the tie by choosing the "mate" who most equally matches the contestant in height.

> **SPECIAL EFFECTS**
>
> If you made a "just married" banner or car decorations, drape these over the winners. If you brought a wedding cake, have the winners be the first to share a piece.

Say: **Congratulations! We've saved you tons of time and confusion in finding your perfect mate. It's obvious that you two will make a great couple since you have so much in common. You can sit down now, too.**

Ask:
- *What do you think about this method of matching mates?*
- *What might be more important to a relationship's success than having some things in common?*
- *What factors do you consider when deciding whether to date someone? Why those factors?*

Say: **We're going to explore dating relationships tonight—what God has to say about them and what you can do now to build a fulfilling, romantic, wonderful marriage in your future. Let's begin by watching Landon and Jamie's relationship in** *A Walk to Remember.*

The Production—*A Walk to Remember*

Gather everyone around the TV to watch the movie. Start the film, sit back, relax, and enjoy!

Postproduction

Building the Perfect Spouse

When the movie ends, allow a five-minute break. After five minutes, call everyone together again. Have teenagers form groups of three or four.

Ask: • *How did this movie make you feel?*

• *What did you like about Landon and Jamie's relationship? What did you not like?*

• *Do you think Jamie was foolish to wait for marriage to have sex since she was terminally ill? Why or why not?*

Reveal the pieces of newsprint with the "female" and "male" symbols on them, then distribute a "Building the Perfect Mate" handout (p. 96) to each person. Say: **Since the Mating Game proved similarities don't guarantee a successful relationship, let's identify the characteristics of the perfect man or woman. The only criteria for our lists are that all the guys must agree on the traits of a perfect woman and all the girls must agree on the traits of a perfect man. Write down the answers on your handout to keep for future reference.**

Spend five minutes on each sex, writing answers on the newsprint. If the guys or girls can't reach a unanimous agreement, take a vote to arrive at least two traits. Afterward, have students discuss these questions with a partner:

• *What are you doing in your own character to develop the traits you seek in others?*

• *How might developing these traits in your own character affect your future dating or marital relationships?*

Say: **When it comes to relationships, people often focus on what they want from the other person. Instead, God wants us to focus on what we can do to serve that person. Paul lays it all out in 1 Corinthians 13, which was quoted at Jamie and Landon's wedding. It's known as the "love" chapter.**

Ask partners to read 1 Corinthians 13 and then discuss these questions:

• *How does this passage compare to the popular view of love and dating?*

• *How would living out this verse in your dating relationships change how you date?*

• *Do you think it's odd that sex isn't mentioned in a chapter about love? Why do you think sex wasn't mentioned?*

Have partners read Matthew 6:25-33 and discuss how the passage relates to dating.

Say: **Jesus tells us not to worry about tomorrow because God knows and answers our needs. Don't worry! By focusing on becoming a man or woman of God, you'll be ready to meet the person with these qualities someday.**

Leggo My Spouse, Oh!

Direct teenagers toward the table where you placed the blocks. Ask them to find two pieces that go together.

Say: **One of the building blocks represents you, and the other represents your high school sweetheart. You've dated exclusively for two years, you're deeply in love, and it's prom night. You decide to have sex. Please fill one of your Lego pieces with super glue and squish the two pieces together, holding them tight.**

While waiting for the glue to dry, have teenagers discuss the following questions with a nearby partner:

• *What physical and emotional reasons do people give for having sex?*

• *How does sex physically and emotionally connect people, even after they break up?*

• *Is it morally acceptable for you to have sex with someone you love? Why or why not?*

Read aloud 1 Corinthians 6:18 to the group. Ask partners to discuss this question:

• *Do you believe premarital sex is as destructive as this verse makes it out to be? Why or why not?*

After several minutes of discussion, say: **Remember what these building blocks represent. You're out of college now. You broke up with your high school sweetheart a long time ago, and you've met the person you're going to marry. It's time for you to break the bond you made with your high school sweetheart.**

Have students try to separate their building blocks, using a screwdriver or hammer if necessary. Read aloud Matthew 19:4-6 as they work, then have them discuss these questions with their partners:

• *How does it feel to break apart the pieces?*

• *How is this breaking apart illustrative of breaking up with a sexual partner?*

• *What negative consequences can come from engaging in premarital sex?*

Say: **Sexual desire is a natural drive God placed within us, and that can make it difficult to wait until marriage. But God put a limit on premarital sex** because sex creates physical, emotional, and spiritual bonds between two people.

Sex is a gift to save for your husband or wife. Look at your Lego. Is this the gift you would want to give to your spouse, the person you love so much that you're going to spend the rest of your life with him or her? Your decisions about dating today have a direct effect on your future happiness.

And we should also understand that there is no judgment or condemnation for people who have had premarital sex; God gives hope to everyone who commits to waiting for the gift of sex at the right time.

Word of Mouth

Love Letter

Say: Before we leave, let's spend a few more minutes thinking about our future spouses. On your "Building the Perfect Mate" handout is a place for you to write a love letter. Think about your future husband or wife, what you're going to do for that person now before you even know who he or she is, and what you hope to do as a couple together someday. You will wait patiently, trusting in Psalm 40:1-3.

Have a volunteer read Psalm 40:1-3 aloud.

Say: Waiting to get married and waiting to have sex can seem like you're stuck in quicksand. God knows and he will give you a new song, a love that lasts a lifetime if you will patiently wait. Be sure to write the date on your letter! It will make a special gift to that person some day.

When you finish, you're free to go. Thanks for coming to the wedding!

Suggested Overnight Retreat Schedule

If you'd like to extend this event into an overnight retreat, use this schedule as a starting point.

Day	Time	Activities	Supplies
Friday	7:00 p.m.-7:30 p.m.	Seat guests	
	7:30 p.m.-9:15 p.m.	*A Walk to Remember*	Movie: *A Walk to Remember*, DVD player or VCR, TV
	9:15 p.m.-9:45 p.m.	Wedding Reception	
	9:45 p.m.-10:00 p.m.	Debriefing	
	10:00 p.m.-11:30 p.m.	Free time	
	Midnight	Lights out	
Saturday	8:00 a.m.-8:30 a.m.	Devotion	
	8:30 a.m.-9:00 a.m.	Breakfast	
	9:00 a.m.-10:00 a.m.	*The Mating Game*	"The Mating Game" handout (p.95), scissors, pens or pencils
		Building the Perfect Mate	Bibles, newsprint, marker, tape, "Building the Perfect Mate" handout (p. 96), pens or pencils
	10:00 a.m.-noon	Games or group activities	
	Noon-1:00 p.m.	Lunch	
	1:00 p.m.-3:00 p.m.	Free time	
	3:00 p.m.-4:00 p.m.	*Leggo My Spouse, Oh!*	Bible, Lego blocks, super glue, hammers, screwdrivers
		Love Letter	"Love Letter" handout (p. 96), pens or pencils
	4:00 p.m.-5:00 p.m.	Free time	
	5:00 p.m.-6:00 p.m.	Dinner	
	6:00 p.m.-7:30 p.m.	Worship and prayer	
	7:30 p.m.-8:00 p.m.	Pack and leave	

The Mating Game

Landon and Jamie welcome you to their nuptials!

Please answer the following questions:

1. What color is your hair?

2. In what month were you born?

3. What school do you attend?

Landon and Jamie welcome you to their nuptials!

Please answer the following questions:

1. What color is your hair?

2. In what month were you born?

3. What school do you attend?

Landon and Jamie welcome you to their nuptials!

Please answer the following questions:

1. What color is your hair?

2. In what month were you born?

3. What school do you attend?

Landon and Jamie welcome you to their nuptials!

Please answer the following questions:

1. What color is your hair?

2. In what month were you born?

3. What school do you attend?

Landon and Jamie welcome you to their nuptials!

Please answer the following questions:

1. What color is your hair?

2. In what month were you born?

3. What school do you attend?

Landon and Jamie welcome you to their nuptials!

Please answer the following questions:

1. What color is your hair?

2. In what month were you born?

3. What school do you attend?

Building the Perfect Mate

Matthew 6:25-33

Love Letter

Today's Date:

Dear Spouse,
I don't know who you are yet, but I'm thinking
about you right now.

Psalm 40:1-3